The Funniest People in Books: 250 Anecdotes

David Bruce

Published by David Bruce, 2022.

While every precaution has been taken in the preparation of this book, the publisher assumes no responsibility for errors or omissions, or for damages resulting from the use of the information contained herein.

THE FUNNIEST PEOPLE IN BOOKS: 250 ANECDOTES

First edition. September 27, 2022.

Copyright © 2022 David Bruce.

ISBN: 979-8215552209

Written by David Bruce.

Table of Contents

Dedication

Dedicated to Carl Eugene Bruce and Josephine Saturday Bruce

My father, Carl Eugene Bruce, died on 24 October 2013. He used to work for Ohio Power, and at one time, his job was to shut off the electricity of people who had not paid their bills. He sometimes would find a home with an impoverished mother and some children. Instead of shutting off their electricity, he would tell the mother that she needed to pay her bill or soon her electricity would be shut off. He would write on a form that no one was home when he stopped by because if no one was home he did not have to shut off their electricity.

The best good deed that anyone ever did for my father occurred after a storm that knocked down many power lines. He and other linemen worked long hours and got wet and cold. Their feet were freezing because water got into their boots and soaked their socks. Fortunately, a kind woman gave my father and the other linemen dry socks to wear.

My mother, Josephine Saturday Bruce, died on 14 June 2003. She used to work at a store that sold clothing. One day, an impoverished mother with a baby clothed in rags walked into the store and started shoplifting in an interesting way: The mother took the rags off her baby and dressed the infant in new clothing. My mother knew that this mother could not afford to buy the clothing, but she helped the mother dress her baby and then she watched as the mother walked out of the store without paying.

***

The doing of good deeds is important. As a free person, you can choose to live your life as a good person or as a bad person. To be a good person, do good deeds. To be a bad person, do bad deeds. If you do good deeds, you will become good. If you do bad deeds, you will become bad. To become the person you want to be, act as if you already are that kind of person. Each of us chooses what kind of person we will become. To become a good person, do the things a good person does. To become a bad person, do the things a bad person does. The opportunity to take action to become the kind of person you want to be is yours.

Human beings have free will. According to the Babylonian Niddah 16b, whenever a baby is to be conceived, the Lailah (angel in charge of contraception) takes the drop of semen that will result in the conception and asks God, "Sovereign of the Universe, what is going to be the fate of this drop? Will it develop into a robust or into a weak person? An intelligent or a stupid person? A wealthy or a poor person?" The Lailah asks all these questions, but it does not ask, "Will it develop into a righteous or a wicked person?" The answer to that question lies in the decisions to be freely made by the human being that is the result of the conception.

A Buddhist monk visiting a class wrote this on the chalkboard: "EVERYONE WANTS TO SAVE THE WORLD, BUT NO ONE WANTS TO HELP MOM DO THE DISHES." The students laughed, but the monk then said, "Statistically, it's highly unlikely that any of you will ever have the opportunity to run into a burning orphanage and rescue an infant. But, in the smallest gesture of kindness — a warm smile, holding the door for the person behind you, shoveling the driveway of the elderly person next door — you have committed an act of immeasurable profundity, because to each of us, our life is our universe."

In her book titled *I Have Chosen to Stay and Fight*, comedian Margaret Cho writes, "I believe that we get complimentary snack-size portions of the afterlife, and we all receive them in a different way." For Ms. Cho, many of her snack-size portions of the afterlife come in hip hop music. Other people get different snack-size portions of the afterlife, and we all must be on the lookout for them when they come our way. And perhaps doing good deeds and experiencing good deeds are snack-size portions of the afterlife.

Cover Photograph for *The Funniest People in Books: 250 Anecdotes*

Photographer: Allen Graham

Agency: Dreamstime.com

All anecdotes have been retold in my own words to avoid plagiarism.

Anecdotes are usually short humorous stories. Sometimes they are thought-provoking or informative, not amusing.

CHAPTER 1: From Advertising to Comedians

Advertising

• While working as an advertising writer for Macy's, Margaret Fishback discovered that the famous department store had a two-foot cake tester on sale. She thought that the idea of a two-foot cake tester was ridiculous, so she wrote, "This cake tester will come in handy the next time you bake a cake two feet high." However, this advertisement brought in more orders than Macy's had two-foot cake testers. From this experience, Ms. Fishback and Macy's learned that humor sells.[1]

• Simon and Schuster once published a children's book by Helen Gaspard titled *Dr. Dan the Bandage Man*. As a publicity gimmick, they decided to include a half-dozen band-aids in each book, so publisher Richard Simon sent this telegram to a friend at Johnson and Johnson: "PLEASE SHIP TWO MILLION BAND-AIDS IMMEDIATELY." The following day Mr. Simon received this telegram in reply: "BAND-AIDS ON THEIR WAY. WHAT THE HELL HAPPENED TO YOU?"[2]

• When horror writer Stephen King decided to live in England for a year, he knew exactly the kind of house he wanted to live in, so he put this advertisement in an English newspaper: "Wanted, a draughty Victorian house in the country with dark attic and creaking floorboards, preferably haunted."[3]

• G.K. Chesterton visited Broadway and Times Square at night when the scene was brightly lit by advertising signs. He gazed at the sight for a while, then said to a friend, "How beautiful it would be for someone who could not read."[4]

Alcohol

• In their book, *The Perfect London Walk*, writers Roger Ebert (the movie critic) and Daniel Curley (a short-story writer) describe what they consider to be the best walk in London — one that lasts for hours and takes the walker through the Hampstead Heath, the Spaniards Inn, Highgate Cemetery, etc. However, Mr. Curley warns the reader that the walk will take you past several pubs, and so you may be tempted away from your walk. In one memorable case, a man named John McHugh stopped at a pub and abandoned the walk after covering scarcely 150 yards.[5]

• While traveling abroad, Mark Twain heard of an American student who had struggled to learn German for three whole months, but who had learned to say only "*zwei glas*," which means "two glasses" (of beer). Still, the student reflected, he had learned those words very thoroughly.[6]

• Percy Hammond, the drama critic, grew up in Cadiz, Ohio, in the late 19th century. One of his favorite memories was marching in a temperance parade as a small child and carrying a banner inscribed with this slogan: "Tremble, King Alcohol, for I shall grow up."[7]

Animals

• As a teenager, Gary Paulsen, author of the young adult novel *Hatchet*, was the favorite victim of a bullying street gang. Late one night, as he left his job at a bowling alley, he tried to find a new route home by leaving from the roof. As he climbed from the roof into an alley, he stepped on a ferocious dog. Frightened, he threw the dog half of a hamburger he was carrying, then he ran from the alley — right into the hands of members of the bullying street gang, who immediately started to beat him. Suddenly, the ferocious dog jumped out of the alley and began biting gang members. Gary gave the dog the rest of his hamburger, and after the dog bit the gang leader in another encounter, the gang left Gary strictly alone. (Eventually, Gary found the dog, now friendly to everyone except Gary's enemies, a new life on a farm.)[8]

• E.B. White may be most famous for his children's book *Charlotte's Web*, in which a spider named Charlotte befriends a pig named Wilbur and saves his life by writing words in her web. The idea for the book came partly from Mr. White's discomfort at raising a pig each year at his farm in Maine, only to butcher it when it was fully grown. In addition, one day he noticed a spider building a web in an outhouse, so he brought out a lamp and a long extension cord and watched the spider. From these experiences, and more, came *Charlotte's Web*. By the way, sometimes people try to find hidden meanings in *Charlotte's Web*, but Mr. White says, "Any attempt to find allegorical meanings is bound to end disastrously, for no meanings are in there. I ought to know."[9]

• Pioneer life could be difficult. In 1875, Laura Ingalls Wilder, author of *Little House on the Prairie*, was outside when she thought she saw a storm spring up on the horizon, then move closer. It wasn't a storm — it was a cloud of grasshoppers. While Laura and her family hid in their house, the grasshoppers ate everything green, including the crops, the garden, the grass, and even the leaves in the trees. After eating everything, the grasshoppers moved west. Because the grasshoppers had destroyed his crops, Laura's Pa walked 200 miles to eastern Minnesota to find work to support his family.[10]

• John Steinbeck, author of *The Grapes of Wrath*, once left a setter puppy named Toby alone for a few hours. Unfortunately, he left Toby alone with a manuscript. By the time Mr. Steinbeck returned to the room, Toby had destroyed half of the only copy of the manuscript — two months' worth of writing. Nevertheless, Mr. Steinbeck did not become upset, saying later, "I didn't want to ruin a good dog for a manuscript I'm not sure is good at all." Instead, he sat down and rewrote the manuscript, which was published with this title: *Of Mice and Men*.[11]

• In New York City, a photographer asked humorist Erma Bombeck to move slightly. She moved where the photographer wanted her to go, then posed — but the photographer had wanted her to move out of the way so he could photograph a dog that was appearing in the movie *Down and Out in Beverly Hills*.[12]

Autographs

• R.L. Stine, the writer of the *Fear Street* and *Goosebumps* children's book series, started out as a writer of comedy; for a while, he edited Scholastic's humor magazine, which was titled *Bananas*. When his first book for children, *How to Be Funny*, was published, he went to a book signing, at which he wore rabbit ears. During the entire afternoon of the book signing, he autographed exactly one book.[13]

• Being a best-selling author can be hazardous to one's health. Horror writer Stephen King spoke at a library in Truth or Consequences, New Mexico, then he signed hundreds of autographs. Even so, some people were not able to get their books autographed — Mr. King's hand developed so many blisters that he was forced to stop signing his autograph.[14]

• In 1975, Quentin Crisp's book *The Naked Civil Servant*, was published, and this very out and very effeminate gay man became a celebrity. Suddenly, taxi drivers who had driven by him even though their taxi was empty not only stopped for him, but they also began to ask for his autograph, saying, "The wife's never going to believe this!"[15]

• Saul Bellow and his wife had an argument one day, so she threw several eight-by-ten glossy photographs of him in the garbage. A few days later, a knock sounded on his door. Standing in the doorway was the porter. He was holding one of the glossy photographs, and he asked Mr. Bellow to sign it.[16]

Automobiles

• Michael Moore, author of *Stupid White Men* and a native of Flint, Michigan, drove Toyotas and Volkswagens. Occasionally, a friend would ask him why he didn't buy a car that was built in the USA. When that happened, Mr. Moore would have his friend open the hood of his "USAmerican" car, and then he'd show his friend that the engine had a sticker saying, "MADE IN BRAZIL" and the fan belt bore the lettering "MADE IN MEXICO." In addition, the radio had a label saying, "MADE IN SINGAPORE."[17]

• Noted author C.G. Norris developed engine trouble and was standing helplessly by his car on the side of a road when a teenage boy came pedaling up to him on his bike. The teenage boy lifted the hood, fiddled with the engine for about 15 seconds, then started the car right up. Mr. Norris looked at the boy and asked, "Do you know what a split infinitive is?" The teenage boy admitted that he didn't, and Mr. Norris said, "Thank God!"[18]

• Children's book author/illustrator David McPhail sometimes writes as he drives. Actually, that's not quite true. He will think of a couple of sentences while driving, then stop the car and write the sentences down. While he was writing *The Cereal Box*, a trip that usually took 90 minutes turned into a three-and-a-half-hour trip.[19]

Books

• In 1922, playwright Lillian Hellman graduated from high school, and her Uncle Jake gave her a ring as her graduation gift. Ms. Hellman, however, cared little for rings, so she sold it for $25 and used the money to buy something she really cared for — books. Later, she told her uncle that she had sold his gift to buy books. He looked at her for a moment, then said, "So you've got spirit after all. Most of the rest of them are made of sugar water."[20]

• As a boy, critic Orville Prescott very quickly learned to love books. While attending a dude ranch that was laughingly called a "school," he was startled by the shout of "Fire!" At first he was pleasantly excited — until he discovered that his own cabin was burning. At that point, he startled everyone by rushing inside the cabin and coming out with an armload of singed books. The astonished onlookers burst into applause.[21]

• During a dinner Cyril Clemens had with G.K. Chesterton, the question of "If one were stranded on a desert island, what book would one like to have?" came up. Mr. Chesterton answered, "If I were a politician who wanted to impress his constituents, I would take Plato or Aristotle, but if I did not want to show off, I would take Thomas' *Guide to Practical Shipbuilding* so that I could get away from the island as quickly as possible."[22]

• In the 1800s, many people did their own doctoring. A book titled *Dr. Gunn's Domestic Medicine* even explained how to perform an amputation, saying that "any man, unless he was a fool or an idiot, could amputate an arm or a leg." First, you needed the book and a few instruments. In addition, since this was in the days before anesthesia, you needed "half a dozen men to hold the victim down."[23]

• A man had the opportunity to publish Mark Twain's first book, *The Celebrated Jumping Frog of Calaveras County, and Other Sketches*, but declined it. Years later, the man chanced to meet Mr. Twain, and told him, "I refused a book of yours and for this I stand without competitor as the prize ass of the 19th century."[24]

• After Lord Avebury published a list of what he regarded as the 100 Best Books, Oscar Wilde was asked to name the books that would appear on his own list of the 100 best books ever written. Mr. Wilde replied, "I fear that would be impossible." When he was asked why, he replied, "Because I have written only five."[25]

Censorship

• Civil rights leader W.E.B. Du Bois was harassed by the United States government. During the Communist scare of the 1950s, the federal government refused to renew his passport unless he signed a statement stating that he did not hold membership in the Communist Party. Mr. Du Bois declined to sign the statement, and he protested to the passport officials, "My beliefs are none of your business. I repeat my demand for a passport in accordance with the Constitution of the United States, the laws of the land, and the decision of the courts." Eventually, the Supreme Court ruled that requiring people to sign such an oath as Mr. Du Bois had been asked to sign before he could get a passport was against the Constitution, and Mr. Du Bois was able to travel abroad again. Even inside the United States, Mr. Du Bois had been censored. He had wanted to speak at a rally sponsored by the American Labor Party on Long Island, New York, but local officials would not let him because they felt that he was a Communist. Interestingly, Mr. Du Bois joined the Communist Party in 1961 — partly in response to the way he had been treated when people thought he was a member of the Communist Party.[26]

• James Joyce's *Ulysses* was almost never published. Portions of *Ulysses* had been published in America in the *Little Review*, but the New York Society for the Suppression of Vice filed charges of obscenity against its publishers, Margaret Anderson and Jane Heap, who were subsequently convicted and forbidden to publish any more excerpts of *Ulysses* in their magazine. Meanwhile, in England Harriet Weaver wanted to publish *Ulysses* but was unable to find a printer who was willing to set the book in type. Fortunately, Mr. Joyce met Sylvia Beach of Shakespeare and Company in Paris, who plunged into publishing the book although she had no experience. How scandalous was *Ulysses* thought to be? On the floor of the Senate, Senator Reed Smoot of Utah said that he had spent 10 minutes skimming the book and that 10 minutes was "enough to indicate that it was written by a man with a diseased mind and soul so black that he would even obscure the darkness of Hell."[27]

• Many citizens of the USSR hated the government and consequently hated the works of propaganda that praised the government. That meant that many people read underground literature instead of the literature officially approved by the government. In one underground joke, a husband discovered that his wife was typing Tolstoy's classic novel *Anna Karenina* and asked her why, since the novel was in print. "Yes," his wife replied, "but you know our son will not read anything that has been published."[28]

• As a young woman, ballerina Margot Fonteyn wished to educate herself and so she read many books, including James Joyce's *Ulysses*, which was banned in Britain when she read it. While she was reading the novel on a bus, ballerina Ninette De Valois asked what she was reading, then almost had a heart attack after seeing the title. She told young Margot, "For God's sake, child, don't read that in public — you could be arrested!"[29]

• L. Frank Baum's books, including *The Wonderful Wizard of Oz*, have occasionally been censored. In 1957, Ralph Ulveling, the Detroit Library Director, ordered the book taken off library shelves because, he charged, it had a "cowardly approach to life." The *Detroit Times* had an interesting response — it serialized the children's novel, adding a notation that this book had been banned.[30]

Children

• Zelda Fitzgerald, the wife of F. Scott, was named after a character — a gypsy queen — in a novel. Throughout her life, she liked to have attention drawn to her. When she was a little girl, she telephoned the fire department, told them that a little girl was stuck on a roof, and gave her own address. She then hung up the telephone, crawled out on the roof, and enjoyed all the commotion she had created. When she was a young unmarried woman, her house was still the center of commotion — young military pilots used to perform aerial stunts over her house to get her attention.[31]

• While attending school in Berkeley, California, Yoshiko Uchida was a member of the Girl Reserves, along with several white girls. One day, a photographer from the local newspaper arrived to take a photo of the Girl Reserves, and he tried to move Yoshiko out of the photo. Fortunately, a white friend, Sylvia, saw what was happening and said, "Come on, Yoshi. Stand next to me." The two friends linked arms and stood firmly together, forcing the photographer to photograph them. Later, Ms. Uchida became the renowned author of *Journey to Topaz*, which is about her experiences as an 11-year-old child in an internment camp for Japanese aliens and citizens in the USA.[32]

• The first of the two most important events in Orville Prescott's life (the other was becoming daily book critic for *The New York Times* in 1942) occurred when he was six years old and his Grandmother Sherwin offered him a $5 gold piece if he would learn how to read. Although he didn't quite know what a $5 gold piece was, he knew that it was desirable, and therefore, a few days later, he read a few pages out of a first-grade primer to his grandmother and received his rewards — the $5 gold piece and the discovery of the joy of reading.[33]

• Playwright Lillian Hellman was born in 1905, and she was a young girl when the United States fought Germany in World War I. Determined to help the war effort, she and a friend went looking for German spies in Manhattan. They spotted two men wearing raincoats. One of the men carried a violin case, which young Lillian thought might hold a machine gun. She reported the two men to a police officer, who investigated and discovered that the two men were a concert violinist and a college professor.[34]

• In addition to being a practical joker, Hugh Troy was a writer and illustrator of children's books. Often, he made up series of stories to tell his little niece. One series starred the popular child actress Shirley Temple, but eventually Mr. Troy got tired of his heroine, so he ended the series by having Shirley Temple run over by a steamroller and flattened like a pancake. His niece loved the ending.[35]

• As a school child, Madeleine L'Engle Camp entered one of her poems in a school contest. She won first prize, only to have a teacher accuse her of plagiarizing the poem. Young Madeleine's mother successfully defended her by showing the teacher other poems and stories that Madeleine had written. As a grownup, Madeleine became famous as Madeleine L'Engle, the author of *A Wrinkle in Time*.[36]

• Henry Wadsworth Longfellow was a poet so popular for such a long time that schoolchildren were made to memorize and recite such poems of his as "The Village Blacksmith" and "Paul Revere's Ride." In the old days, a schoolchild who heard a friend accidentally make a rhyme would say, "You're a poet and don't know it, but your big feet show it — they're long fellows!"[37]

• Oscar Wilde's two boys, Cyril and Vyvyan, preferred to dress in sailor suits, but Mr. Wilde and his wife often dressed them in Little Lord Fauntleroy costumes, especially before showing them off to guests in the drawing room. The boys objected to this, so one day they stripped off the costumes and pranced stark naked into the drawing room.[38]

• The *Curious George* children's books about an inquisitive monkey are written and illustrated by H.A. Rey. Children got so involved with the main character of the book that they were sometimes disappointed when they met Mr. and Mrs. Rey. One small, disappointed boy told them, "I thought you were monkeys, too."[39]

• When she was very small, children's book author Patricia McKissack toured the house of a former President during a field trip. Later, she was asked to describe what she had seen to a PTA group. Young Patricia reported that her personal guides for the tour had been a rabbit and a mouse.[40]

• When F. Scott Fitzgerald, author of *The Great Gatsby*, was seven years old, he invited some children to come to his birthday party, and he was very disappointed when no one showed up for the party. To make up for his disappointment, his mother let him eat all of the birthday cake.[41]

• When L. Frank Baum, author of the Oz books, was traveling in Egypt, he met a little Algerian girl who had traveled across the desert with her family on camel. Her family had allowed her to choose one book to bring with her, and she had chosen *The Wonderful Wizard of Oz*.[42]

• Some children are more precocious than others. When he was age 12, Edward Albee had already written his first three-act play, *Aliqueen* — it was a sex farce.[43]

• Hilaire Belloc wrote quickly and published much. When asked why he wrote so quickly, he replied, "Because my children are howling for pearls and caviar."[44]

Christmas

• When nonconformist American poet Emily Dickinson was a teenager attending the Mount Holyoke Seminary in South Hadley, Massachusetts, the head of the school, Miss Mary Lyon, told the students that Christmas would be celebrated in a spiritual way. The students would fast in their rooms and pray all day without eating. Miss Lyon then asked the students to stand if they agreed with her plan. Ms. Dickinson remained seated. After the students had sat down again, Miss Lyon asked any students to stand if they disagreed with her plan. Ms. Dickinson was the only student who stood.[45]

• The parents of Jerry Spinelli, author of the Newbery Medal-winning *Maniac Magee*, spent very little money on themselves, but out of love they made sure that their children enjoyed very nice Christmases. One Christmas, Jerry had unwrapped what he thought was his final present. His father told him, "Well, I guess that's it. Looks like you did pretty good this year." Later, Jerry was sent on an errand to the kitchen, and he found his real final present: a Roadmaster bicycle. Mr. Spinelli describes the gift in a memorable way: "Love leaning on a kickstand."[46]

Comedians

• When visiting Robert Graves, comedian Terry-Thomas felt that perhaps he had offended the famous poet with his sense of over-confidence because instead of having an intellectual discussion about Greek mythology, all Mr. Graves talked to him about was compost, frequently sticking a fork into various maturing piles and making Terry-Thomas smell them.[47]

• Anne Beatts, a writer for *Saturday Night Live*, used to keep a hospital bed in her office at Rockefeller Center. She used it for writing (her typewriter sat where the food tray would normally sit), instead of a desk and chair.[48]

CHAPTER 2: From Couples to Fans

Couples

• At age 40, children's book author Lois Lowry got divorced and started dating, a process she hated, mostly because the men who took her out told her things like they had a wife but were thinking seriously of getting divorced or they had a problem with alcohol but were thinking seriously of quitting drinking. One day, she wore an expensive dress on a date with a rich man who opened the door on what she thought was the driver's side of his car and motioned for her to get in. She said, "I'd really prefer that you drive," and he replied, "I'm going to. The steering wheel's on the other side of a Rolls [Rolls-Royce]." Later, she was watching an episode of *Kate and Allie* when one of the stars took out a dress from a closet — the same dress that she had been wearing on the date with the rich man — and the other star made fun of it. After that, she still wore the dress, but she didn't like it as much. Fortunately, on another date she met another man, Martin, who quoted the Babar the Elephant books and who grew a beard after she said that she preferred men who had beards.[49]

• Pulitzer Prize-winning reporter Meyer Berger used to do odd jobs around the house while thinking about how to write an article. One day, the deadline was approaching for a difficult magazine article, so his wife decided to leave him at home so he could write. She entertained some visitors, taking them to a movie and dinner, and when she returned, she discovered that her husband hadn't typed a single word — but he had polished the silver and run the vacuum cleaner. However, the time spent doing housework was also time spent planning the article. The next day, Mr. Meyer sat down before the typewriter and quickly wrote a very good article.[50]

• As a young man, Dean Koontz kept writing novels and also worked to earn a living, but although he published some books, his writing career seemed to be going nowhere. His wife, Gerda, saw that her husband was worried, so she offered to support him for five years as he wrote, saying, "If you can't make it in five years, you never will." Mr. Koontz accepted her offer, and after quitting his job, he started writing for sixty hours a week. At the end of the five years, Mr. Koontz had succeeded to such an extent that his wife quit her job to manage the business end of her husband's writing career.[51]

• When Kate Mostel and Madeline Gilford decided to write a book of autobiography and anecdotes in conjunction with their famous husbands, Zero Mostel and Jack Gilford, Mr. Mostel was reluctant at first and thought his wife was wasting her time, but after reading a few pages of her writing, he became enthusiastic. In fact, he made a writing room for Kate in their home, and he bought her a writing desk. When a salesman showed him a little writing desk, he said, "No, no. That's too small. We need a serious writing desk. My wife's a writer."[52]

• Humorist H. Allen Smith made a trip with his wife to visit places he had lived at as a young man. He and his wife went to visit a dance club where Mr. Smith had very happy memories of squiring his girlfriends. They discovered that the dance club had been torn down and its foundation was in the middle of a pasture where a goat was grazing. Mr. Smith's wife told him, "I see one of your old girlfriends is left."[53]

• English critic Sir Max Beerbohm and his aging wife went to a party. Sir Max was immediately surrounded by many beauties who wanted to impress him, but as soon as it was proper for him to leave the party, he turned to his wife and said, "Darling, let's go to a restaurant and find a quiet corner. You are looking so charming tonight that I want to talk to you alone."[54]

• Beatrice Kaufman, the wife of witty playwright George S., was witty in her own right. While playing the game "Ask Me Another," she was asked, "Who wrote *The Virginian*?" Having correctly answered "Owen Wister," she was asked the next question, "Who wrote *The*

Virginians?" This time she answered "Owens Wisters." (The correct answer is William Makepeace Thackeray.)[55]

• G.K. Chesterton was disorganized in his personal life, and he relied on his wife to keep track of his appointments. One day, he sent her a telegram: "AM IN MARKET HARBOROUGH. WHERE OUGHT I TO BE?" She wired him back: "HOME."[56]

• Gail Parent writes comedy, which has occasionally led to problems. While she was in college, a suitor gave her one perfect rose. She ruined what could have been a tender romantic moment by asking, "Where are the other eleven?"[57]

Critics

• Pat Hutchins wrote a children's book titled *The Mona Lisa Mystery*, in which someone smuggles the famous painting from the museum by wrapping it around a leg then wrapping a bandage over the painting. After the book was published, a child wrote her to say that the painting could not be smuggled out of the museum in that way — the *Mona Lisa* is painted on wood. Ms. Hutchins did some extra research and discovered that the child was right.[58]

• The Ukrainian playwright O.E. Korneychuk wrote plays praising the Communists of the USSR. In one underground joke, Comrade Korneychuk said that he had put a lot of fire into his new play. A theater-goer replied, "It would have been better if it had been the other way around."[59]

• Ballerina Margot Fonteyn was so famous that she had huge numbers of press clippings, most of which she neglected to read. However, one notice did give her special satisfaction: "Margot Fonteyn, who has triumphed in many more exotic places, last night conquered Flatbush."[60]

• Dorothy Parker — who signed her book reviews in *The New Yorker* as "Constant Reader" — disliked cutesy children's books. She wrote this review of A.A. Milne's *House at Pooh Corner*: "Tonstant Weader fwowed up."[61]

• Walter Savage Landor enjoyed criticizing many, many things. Once he even criticized the Psalms! Hearing this, a friend of his, Marguerite, Countess Blessington, smiled and said, "Do write something better, Mr. Landor."[62]

• After being barred from seeing the opening of a play, columnist Walter Winchell wrote that he would wait three days and see the play's closing.[63]

Death

• While traveling, Mark Twain and his friends tortured irritating tour guides by constantly asking if someone was dead. For example, when a tour guide showed them a bust of Christopher Columbus, they would ask, "Is he dead?" Once, Mr. Twain and friends visited the Capuchin Cemetery, where the bones of dead monks were used to make arches and other ornaments. One of the exhibitions of the cemetery was the corpse of a monk who had been dead for 150 years. Mr. Twain decided to cut the tour short because he could tell that his friends were tempted to ask, "Is he dead?"[64]

• Children's author Roald Dahl almost died because of careless instructions. During World War II, he was told to fly to a certain airbase but when he arrived nothing was there because his instructions were off by 50 miles. Low on fuel and with night approaching, he decided to try to land the plane. He crashed, and he suffered serious head injuries. Fortunately, he managed to get out of the plane. The burning plane attracted the attention of some British soldiers and Mr. Dahl was taken to a military hospital.[65]

• Dorothy Parker was cremated after her death. She greatly admired Martin Luther King, Jr., and she bequeathed her estate to the National Association for the Advancement of Colored People. Her ashes are at the headquarters of the NAACP, which dedicated a memorial garden to her memory. The marker in the garden says, "This memorial garden is dedicated to her noble spirit, which celebrated the oneness of humankind and to the bonds of everlasting friendship between black and Jewish people."[66]

• As a man who has spent much time in the wilderness, Gary Paulsen, author of *Hatchet*, has seen corpses of people who have died of many things, including "blatant stupidity." In one remarkable case, a man went cross-country skiing in the dead of winter but neglected to take along matches or a lighter. He broke his leg and froze to death, although enough wood was around him to have kept thousands of people warm.[67]

• Robert Benchley and Charles MacArthur attended the funeral of a friend whose wake had been held in a third-floor walk-up apartment. After the service, the pallbearers picked up the coffin and started to carry it down a twisting staircase that forced them to hold the coffin in a slanted position. Watching them, Mr. Benchley commented, "Oh my, the change will fall out of his pocket."[68]

• A bad man asked Scottish poet Robert Burns to lend him his black coat so he could attend a funeral the following day. Mr. Burns replied that he would be attending that funeral, so he could not lend him his black coat. But he suggested, "I can recommend the most excellent substitute. Throw your character over your shoulders. That will be the blackest coat you ever wore in your lifetime."[69]

• While writing *Roots*, Alex Haley became depressed. He suffered from writer's block, and he traveled on a ship to Africa, hoping that it would help him to write. One night, he thought about throwing himself overboard and drowning, but then he heard the voices of his ancestors, including Kunta Kinte and his grandmother, speak to him and tell him that he had to finish *Roots*.[70]

• Quentin Crisp, author of *The Naked Civil Servant*, could be bitchy when confronted by public displays of grief over the deaths of celebrities whom the mourners did not know. When a crying woman ran into a cafe where Mr. Crisp was sitting and dramatically announced that the Welsh poet Dylan Thomas had died, Mr. Crisp asked, "Was he a relation of yours?"[71]

• Geraldine Farrar's autobiography titled *Such Sweet Compulsion* begins, "I died in the beginning of the year 1923." No, Ms. Farrar did not die then, either emotionally or physically. Her mother died then, and Ms. Farrar wrote her autobiography using both her own voice and that of her mother, who she believed had gone on to a higher plane of existence.[72]

• In her book *Mark Twain in Nevada*, Effie Mona Mack wrote about the cheapness of life in the frontier. In 1863, a man who was shot and died in Virginia City, Nevada, remained under a billiards table from 4 a.m. until noon while frontiersmen continued to shoot billiards above him. The coroner was too busy to come and take away the corpse.[73]

• In Highgate Cemetery in London, many tourists visit the grave of Elizabeth Eleanor Siddal, who was the wife and model of the painter Dante Gabriel Rossetti. When she died in 1862, Rossetti buried some poems with her. However, in 1869, he reconsidered and had her grave dug up so he could retrieve the poems.[74]

• On his deathbed, irreverent playwright Brendan Behan was taken care of by a nun. With his last words, he thanked her, then added, "May you be the mother of a bishop."[75]

Editors

• A young Broadway columnist for the *New York World-Telegram* didn't like the way his column was being edited, so he went to see the copy editor, a Mr. Doyle, and said, "I'm damn well fed up with the way you've been trimming my stuff. After all, this is Broadway stuff I'm writing. You don't know anything about Broadway. You never get around the hot spots. You're not qualified to pass judgment on Broadway topics. Now admit it, Mr. Doyle." Mr. Doyle replied, "You're right. I'm just a country boy. I don't know a thing about Broadway and the night spots. I never been in one of them nightclubs. I don't see

Times Square once a year. I'm a country boy, brought up on a farm, spent most of my life on a farm, and consequently there's only one thing I know. I know horse sh*t when I see it."[76]

• Gertrude Stein was known for her odd style of writing, which provoked this parody in a rejection slip from editor A.J. Fifield: "I am only one, only one, only one. Only one being, one at the same time. Not two, not three, only one. Only one life to live, only sixty minutes in one hour. Only one pair of eyes. Only one brain. Only one being. Being only one, having only one pair of eyes, having only one time, having only one life, I cannot read your MS three or four times. Not even one time. Only one look, only one look is enough. Hardly one copy would sell here. Hardly one. Hardly one."[77]

• A woman sent editor Walter H. Page a story to read, but he sent it back to her saying that it was not suitable for publication in his magazine. The woman then wrote him, saying that he had not read the story because she had glued the corners of a couple of pages together and when the story came back to her, those corners were still glued together. Mr. Page replied to the woman: "Madam, when I get an egg for breakfast, I do not need to eat the whole of it to see that it is bad."[78]

• At a New England Yearly Meeting of Quakers, they debated about the wording of the Discipline. Some people thought that a certain paragraph should perhaps be deleted or altered. One man, however, objected, saying, "I should be sorry to see that paragraph left out, or even changed. Those words seem almost sacred to me." Rufus Jones spoke up and said, "Nothing very sacred about that — I wrote it myself."[79]

Education

• Helene Hanff, author of *84 Charing Cross Road* and *The Duchess of Bloomsbury Street*, got to college through a fluke. Since she was born in 1915, the Depression was raging when she normally would have gone to college, and her parents simply had no money to send her. However, Temple University was offering scholarships, so Miss Hanff took the scholarship exam and failed spectacularly in the map section of the exam. Here's what happened. The History exam was in two parts: Part 1 required written answers and Part 2 was a map test (locating countries, etc., on an unmarked map). Since Miss Hanff's high school History exams had never included map tests, she decided to cram for this part of the test. She got two maps — one of the U.S. and one of Europe — and studied them. Eventually she had them cold, partly by memorizing the color of the countries. Unfortunately, the map on the History test was a black-and-white map of the world, and so Miss Hanff ended up identifying the Pacific Ocean as "Africa." Fortunately, she aced the written part of the test. Because the examining committee was intrigued by the disparity of the scores on the two parts of her test, they interviewed her, found out what had happened, and allowed her to go to college.[80]

• As a cub steamboat pilot on the Mississippi River, Mark Twain was taught a valuable, but embarrassing, lesson by an experienced pilot, Mr. Bixby. Mr. Bixby asked Mark if he knew enough to take the steamboat across the next crossing. Aware that there was plenty of water in the channel and no chance of running aground, Mark replied that of course he could, since "I couldn't get bottom there with a church steeple." Mr. Bixby replied, "You think so, do you?" Something in Mr. Bixby's voice shook Mark's confidence, which Mr. Bixby's leaving Mark alone in the pilothouse did nothing to restore. The crossing did not go smoothly. Mark imagined shallow water and reefs everywhere, and eventually had to be rescued by Mr. Bixby, although there was absolutely no danger of grounding the steamboat. After the ordeal, Mr. Bixby told his protégé, "You shouldn't have allowed me or anybody else to shake your confidence .... Try to remember that. And another thing: when you get into a dangerous place, don't turn coward. That isn't going to help matters any."[81]

• Lorraine Hansberry attended the University of Wisconsin for a while, but dropped out after two years because of a course in Scenic Design. She liked the course, she worked hard in it, and she expected to receive an A. However, when she received her grade report, she discovered that the instructor had given her a failing grade. When she asked why, he explained that a black woman could not succeed in the theater, and he was trying to save her from future disappointment. In 1959, the New York Drama Critics Circle named Ms. Hansberry's *A Raisin in the Sun* the Best Play of the Year.[82]

• When he was a schoolchild, children's book author Walter Dean Myers had a reputation for fighting teachers because one day, he thought he would entertain his schoolmates by pretending to kick his teacher as they walked on a staircase landing. Unfortunately, his teacher paused just as young Walter launched the kick, and instead of narrowly missing the teacher, as he had intended, Walter kicked him squarely in the buttocks. After class, his teacher walked him home, where he began a conversation with his mother by saying, "Mrs. Myers, I had a little problem with Walter that I think you should know about."[83]

• At Columbia University, author Corey Ford was so busy that he didn't have time to read any books for his course in 18th-century literature with Professor Harrison Ross Steeves. Mr. Ford skipped the final examination, then arranged for an oral examination, at which he appeared totally unread and unprepared. After Mr. Ford answered the first question — and got the sex wrong of a major literary character — Professor Steeves handed him a contemporary book to read, then gave him a gentleman's C for the course.[84]

• In his book *A Tramp Abroad*, Mark Twain wrote about the lecture system at Heidelberg, where attendance was not mandatory. Often, only a few students showed up for especially arcane lectures. Mr. Twain told of a lecturer who spoke day after day to an audience consisting of three students. One day, two of the students were away, and only one student showed up for the lecture. The lecturer began his remarks as usual by saying, "Gentlemen," corrected himself and said, "Sir," and then went on with his lecture.[85]

• E.B. White is the famous author of *Charlotte's Web* and many books of essays, and he learned about writing wherever he could, including from his English professor at Cornell, William Strunk, author of a small book titled *Elements of Style*. Another helpful advisor was a Mr. Johns, city editor at the *Seattle Times*. Mr. White was seeking the best way to phrase something, and he asked Mr. Johns for help. Mr. Johns gave him this very good advice: "Just say the words."[86]

• Humorist Robert Benchley attended Harvard, where he became editor of the *Lampoon*. Just before finals, he became very ill. Unable to get out of bed for his International Law final, he had a proctor give him the exam in his bedroom. An essay question on the final concerned the Newfoundland Fisheries case, and he wrote about the case using the point of view of a fish. (Mr. Benchley's professor gave him an F, which kept him from getting a degree at Harvard until later.)[87]

• Show the haters that they are wrong. Robert DeMott and Dave Smith became friends in the early 1970s. They had a number of things in common that facilitated their friendship: they were or would become editors, scholars, teachers, and writers, plus both had been told as undergraduates by professors that they "were not smart enough or able enough to amount to much in the 'real' world" — predictions that they ignored. Mr. DeMott became a noted John Steinbeck scholar, and Mr. Smith became a noted poet.[88]

• When Michael Moore, author of *Stupid White Men*, was in his sophomore year in college, he tried for an hour to find a parking space so he could get out of his car and go to class. After an hour, he gave up and shouted, "That's it — I'm dropping out!" Then he went home and told his parents that he was dropping out of school. When they asked him why, he explained, "I couldn't find a parking space." He never attended class again.[89]

• When Peg Bracken, author of *I Hate to Cook Book*, started writing, she would often type the first page of a famous short story for inspiration. Often, she discovered that the page did not look as impressive typed on a sheet of paper as it did printed on a page in a book, so sometimes she would imitate her English professor and write on the sheet of paper: "You can do better than this, Mr. Faulkner."[90]

• While living in Burr Oak, Iowa, Laura Ingalls Wilder, author of *Little House on the Prairie*, used to live above a grocery store. In the afternoons, she and her sister practiced elocution — reading out loud with feeling — for school. They didn't know it, but grocery store customers used to come by regularly and stand where they could hear the girls read exciting stories and poems.[91]

• When comic writer H. Allen Smith was a youth attending parochial school, he did well in some subjects, but was terrible at accounting. However, he discovered a novel way to improve his accounting grade. After discovering an unlocked window, he used to go to school after hours a few times a week and copy the accounting ledger of grade-A student Helen Weisenburger.[92]

• Leo Rosten, author of *The Joy of Yiddish*, discovered early in his life an easy way to get out of doing his chores: All he had to do was pick up a book and read it. When he was reading something, his parents would do his chores for him rather than interrupt the learning process.[93]

• Lord Byron was asked on an examination about Jesus' miracle of turning water into wine. As other students wrote on and on about the miracle's religious and spiritual meaning, Byron sat quietly for a long time, then wrote, "The water met its Master, and blushed."[94]

Fans

• While writing his young adult novel *I Am the Cheese*, the late Robert Cormier needed to include a telephone number. He worried about making up a telephone number because he knew that people would call it, and the person whose number it was might not like the calls. Therefore, he used his own telephone number. As soon as the novel was published, his telephone started ringing. Over the years, thousands of children and teenagers have called that number and talked to him. Fortunately, Mr. Cormier enjoyed talking to his readers. He acknowledged, "As a writer, I can't afford to be a recluse or not involved with life."[95]

• After the publication of her best-selling book *The Sea Around Us*, environmentalist Rachel Carson became a major celebrity. During a lecture tour in the South, she stopped in a beauty parlor to have her hair done. Suddenly, her hair dryer stopped, and the proprietor of the beauty parlor said, "I hope you don't mind, but there is someone who wants to meet you." She did meet the person, with her still-wet hair up in curlers and a towel wrapped around her neck.[96]

• The poet John Greenleaf Whittier disliked celebrity hunters. One day, he was in a store talking with the owner when a woman came in and asked if he could tell her where the famous poet John Greenleaf Whittier lived. Mr. Whittier pointed to his own house, which was across the street. Then he made sure to keep away from his house until the celebrity hunter had left the vicinity.[97]

• Louisa May Alcott, author of *Little Women*, was a major celebrity in her day. Once, a woman told her, "If you ever come to Oshkosh, your feet will not be allowed to touch the ground — you will be carried in the arms of the people. Will you come?" Ms. Alcott replied, "Never."[98]

• R.L. Stine, author of the *Goosebumps* and *Fear Street* series, has many young fans who enjoy his writing. One nine-year-old boy got Mr. Stine's autograph on a copy of *Monster Blood*. After receiving the autograph, the boy told Mr. Stine, "I'm the luckiest man on earth!"[99]

CHAPTER 3: From Fathers to Marriage

Fathers

• Author Frank DeCaro was such a poor player in Little League baseball that his coach created a new position just for him: roving outfielder. He was stationed in the parking lot because no one could hit a ball that far. After the season was over, Frank told his father that he wanted to quit. Surprised, his father asked why he had begun to play in the first place, and Frank answered that he had done it for him, because he knew that his father wanted a son who played sports. That's when his father said something wise and wonderful: "Don't ever do *anything* just for me."[100]

• Isaac Asimov wrote hundreds of books during his life. His father once looked at one of the many books Mr. Asimov had written and asked, "How did you learn all this, Isaac?" Mr. Asimov replied, "From you. You valued learning, and you taught me to value it. All the rest came without trouble."[101]

• Leo Rosten's father emigrated from Poland to the United States. To learn English, he attended night school, where a teacher asked him for an example of a noun. He answered, "A door." She then asked him for another example of a noun, so he answered, "Another door."[102]

Food

• When Gary Paulsen wrote his novel *Hatchet*, which is about a young boy who finds himself alone in the wilderness with only a hatchet when the person piloting the small plane he is in dies of a heart attack, he wanted the novel to be as realistic as possible. Therefore, whatever the hero, Brian, experiences in the novel, Mr. Paulsen also set out to experience in real life. In doing this, he was remarkably successful, even creating fire using a hatchet and a stone. However, he experienced a setback when he attempted to eat turtle eggs. The eggs so nauseated him that he vomited, despite three valiant attempts to eat them. However, his lead sled dog, Cookie, enjoyed eating the eggs —

she also enjoyed eating his vomit. Despite his lack of success in eating the turtle eggs, Mr. Paulsen decided to leave the egg-eating scene in his novel — he figured that Brian would be so hungry that he would be able to eat the eggs and not vomit.[103]

• One morning, President Theodore Roosevelt sat down to a breakfast of sausages with a book in his hands. The book was *The Jungle*, by Upton Sinclair, and President Roosevelt read, "There was never the least attention paid to what was cut up for sausage ... meat on the floor, in the dirt and sawdust, where workers had tramped and spit uncounted billions of germs ... meat stored in great piles ... and thousands of rats would race about on it." President Roosevelt screamed, "I'M POISONED!" — then he threw his breakfast sausages out a White House window.[104]

• Alex Haley knew that he wanted to be a writer, and he was willing to live in poverty in order to have time to write. While Mr. Haley was living in New York City, a friend offered to give him a job, but he turned it down because he wanted to be a writer. Mr. Haley then took stock of his food supplies, and he discovered that he had only two cans of sardines — and to replenish his food supply, he had only 18 cents. The next day, Mr. Haley sold one of his articles, and he framed the two cans of sardines and the 18 cents. Later, of course, he wrote *Roots*.[105]

• The ancient Greek poet Timokreon was born on the Mediterranean island of Rhodes, but he became the guest of the king of Persia. While sitting at the king's table, Timokreon ate so much that the king of Persia was astonished, but Timokreon explained that he was stuffing himself so he could demonstrate his fighting skill the next day. He made good on his boast, and after defeating several warriors, he started slashing his sword at the air, explaining that he still had many blows left for anyone who wished to fight him.[106]

• While riding the bus home, gay author Michael Thomas Ford heard a couple of teenage boys talking about "faggots" and saying that a certain macrobiotic restaurant the bus had passed was a hangout for "fags." One of the boys says, "All them homos eat that health food sh*t." When Mr. Ford got off the bus at his stop, he first leaned down to the boys and said, "You know, some of us homos eat the same crap you two do."[107]

• In her book on children surviving cancer, *I Want to Grow Hair, I Want to Grow Up, I Want to Go to Boise*, Erma Bombeck wrote about a child who had lost her hair to chemotherapy and was being stared at by some young children in a hospital. The child pulled off her wig as she said, "Hey, you want to see what happens when you don't eat your vegetables?"[108]

• Dr. Seuss wrote *Green Eggs and Ham* after Random House editor Bennett Cerf challenged him to write a children's book using only 50 words. Although he met the challenge, Dr. Seuss says that writing the book did have a disadvantage — afterward, whenever he was invited to a banquet, he was served green eggs and ham.[109]

• When playwright Neil Simon was a child, he told his mother that he liked chocolate pudding, so she made chocolate pudding for dessert 15 days in a row. Finally, he got tired of always eating chocolate pudding for dessert, so he said that he didn't want the pudding. His mother said, "But I thought you liked it."[110]

• Gertrude Stein wrote the autobiography of her friend Alice B. Toklas; however, Ms. Toklas did write the *Alice B. Toklas Cookbook*. This book describes meals with famous painters and authors — it also includes a recipe for Haschich Fudge.[111]

Gays and Lesbians

• When gay author Michael Thomas Ford first lived in New York, he didn't know what to expect when he became involved with the gay scene. During Pride Weekend, he and a lesbian friend went to a gay men's dance on Christopher Street. This turned out to be a mistake, as many of the gay men dancing made it clear that they did not want a woman present. The next year, Mr. Ford was invited to a women's dance during Pride Weekend. Remembering what had happened the previous year, he was nervous about going, but his lesbian friends talked him into it. As he had expected, he was the only man present, and he was plenty nervous when a butch female walked up to him. However, the woman simply shook his hand and told him, "I just want you to know that I'm glad you're here." (So did more than 100 other women, many of whom laughed at the slogan on his T-shirt: "LESBIAN TRAPPED IN A MAN'S BODY.") During the evening, Mr. Ford noticed that the women's dance was very inclusive. Whereas the people at the previous year's men's dance were judged by their looks and their buffness, the people present at the women's dance were of all ages, all colors, all shapes, and all sizes. Even women in wheelchairs were present. The only problem that occurred is that Mr. Ford's lesbian friends got jealous because he was talking to more women than they were.[112]

• The classic "coming out" novel about a lesbian girl is *Rubyfruit Jungle* by Rita Mae Brown. The classic "coming out" autobiography about a gay boy is *The Best Little Boy in the World* by John Reid (then-pseudonym of financial writer Andrew Tobias — now he doesn't use a pseudonym). Despite having different publishers, both books were published in hardback in 1973, and both books were published in paperback in 1977. But for the real coincidence, read this: As children, both Mr. Tobias and Ms. Brown attended summer camp in Maine. Andy went to Camp Wigwam, and Rita Mae went to its sister camp, Camp Hiawatha. On a couple of occasions, the two went to the movies together, double-dating with a couple of older counselors.[113]

• Knowing about the gay community can be reassuring. In Colorado, lesbian humorist Ellen Orleans and her girlfriend were sitting in a park watching a thunderstorm up in the mountains. It got dark, and they started walking to their car, worrying about their safety. They heard a rustle in the bushes and a tall man suddenly stepped out in front of them. Ms. Orleans and her girlfriend saw that he was dressed in leather from head to toe and immediately felt relief — he wasn't a rapist, just a gay man looking for other gay men.[114]

• When gay author Frank DeCaro was interviewed for a job as men's fashion columnist for the *Detroit Free Press*, his editor (who didn't know that Mr. DeCaro is gay) warned him of the job's "faggot factor" — meaning that almost everyone assumes that all men's fashion columnists are gay. Mr. DeCaro replied that he didn't think it would be a problem for him.[115]

• Lesbian author Erika Lopez ran into problems when she visited her grandmother, who was becoming forgetful. Her grandmother kept introducing her to the waiter, Ms. Lopez reminded her grandmother that she is a lesbian, then her grandmother forgot and introduced her to the waiter again. On some days, Ms. Lopez came out to her grandmother 50 times.[116]

• Lesbian author Gail Sausser is tired of reading lesbian novels that have unhappy endings; she strongly prefers a happy ending. Many of her friends are the same way. In fact, one friend always reads the last two paragraphs of any lesbian novel she is considering buying because she wants to make sure it doesn't have an unhappy ending.[117]

• During his time as a prisoner, gay playwright Oscar Wilde stood on a train platform in drizzling rain while handcuffed to two other convicts. He said to one of the police officers escorting him, "Sir, if this is the way Queen Victoria treats her convicts, she doesn't deserve to have any."[118]

• A reader wrote in to Dear Abby to ask, "A pair of gay men is moving in across the street. What can we do to improve the neighborhood?" Dear Abby (Abigail Van Buren) replied, "You could move."[119]

• Liane de Pougy, an author and the lesbian lover of the American poet Natalie Barney, was reputed to say this during confession: "Father, except for murder and robbery I've done everything."[120]

Halloween

• As a house-guest, Dorothy Parker belatedly discovered that her hostess was a rhymes-with-witch. Entering a bathroom, she discovered a female friend of hers, who pointed to a decrepit toothbrush, then asked, "What do you think our hostess does with that?" Ms. Parker said, "I think she rides it on Halloween."[121]

Homes

• American poet Natalie Barney was not known for her housekeeping. Someone once pointed out that her house and furniture were dusty, but she merely replied, "The dust is pretty; it's furniture's face powder!"[122]

• In 1979, after buying a 23-room, 129-year-old mansion in Bangor, Maine, horror writer Stephen King put a fence around it — the fence is decorated with the figures of bats and spiders.[123]

Illness and Injury

• In her book about children surviving cancer, *I Want to Grow Hair, I Want to Grow Up, I Want to Go to Boise*, Erma Bombeck related a story told to her by a father whose daughter had lost a leg to Ewing's sarcoma. His daughter was in a hospital bed and was emotionally depressed. An orderly came with a wheelchair to take her to the X-ray room. The orderly put her in the wheelchair, adjusted the foot that was sticking out, and then began groping for the foot she didn't have. The girl with the missing leg looked at the orderly for a moment, and then smiled and said, "Good luck!"[124]

• When World War I started, G.K. Chesterton wanted to fight for England, but an injury prevented him from raising an arm very high, thus making it impossible for him to join the infantry. In addition, his imposing weight made it impossible for him to join the cavalry. After taking thought of how he could serve his country in war, he said ruefully, "I might possibly form part of a barricade."[125]

Illustrations

• Children's book authors sometimes have odd conversations with the artists who illustrate their books. After looking at *Newsweek* one day, Joanna Cole, author of *The Magic School Bus Lost in the Solar System*, called the book's illustrator, Bruce Degen, to ask, "Bruce, have you painted Neptune yet?" She then told him that *Newsweek* had published some photographs that revealed that Neptune had a Great Dark Spot, something that astronomers had not known about before. Mr. Degen had already painted Neptune, but he was able to easily create a Great Dark Spot with a dab of dark grey paint.[126]

• As a young man, Ludwig Bemelmans, author and illustrator of such children's books as the *Madeline* series, lived in a sparsely furnished apartment. To brighten up the apartment, he painted scenic views on the window shades and pictures of elegant pieces of furniture on the walls.[127]

Insults

• Drama critic Percy Hammond occasionally did not like certain people, and he showed his dislike. After moving from Chicago to New York City, Mr. Hammond was attending a play when its press agent came up to him and asked, "Are you getting to like New York any better, or are you still lonely for Chicago?" Mr. Hammond replied, "Never so acutely as tonight." Another time, Mr. Hammond was tired of the hero worship shown to Stuart Sherman, who became literary editor of the *Herald* after working at the University of Illinois. On hearing that Mr. Sherman was looking for an apartment in New York, Mr. Hammond asked, "Does he want to pay a high rent, or is he content with a walk-up shrine?"[128]

• Unpublished authors sometimes besiege published authors, hoping for free criticisms of their works. A woman brought a play to Samuel Johnson and requested that he read and criticize it. Being already busy with his own work, Dr. Johnson begged off, saying that if she read through it herself with a critical eye, she would find the same mistakes he would. The woman said, "But sir, I have no time — I have already so many irons in the fire." Dr. Johnson replied, "Then, madam, the best thing I can advise you to do is put your tragedy along with your irons."[129]

• Author G.K. Chesterton became annoyed by the noise made by a local film studio located near his house because it interfered with his writing. Eventually, he sent his secretary to complain to the head of the studio. She made a strong protest: "The situation is becoming impossible. ... Mr. Chesterton can't write." The studio head replied, "We were well aware of that."[130]

• In his autobiography, *Ave Atque Vale*, writer George Moore criticized one of his former professors. The professor, Robert Yelverton Tyrrell, responded, "Moore is one of those folks who think that *Atque* [Latin for *and*] was a Roman centurion."[131]

• Oscar Wilde listened to Frank Harris, author of *My Life and Loves*, tell a long story which turned out to be a paraphrase of a story by Anatole France. Afterward, Mr. Wilde said, "What a charming story, Frank. Anatole France would have spoiled it."[132]

Language

• Ian Fleming, the author of the James Bond books, worked for British Naval Intelligence during World War II. Sometimes, he would take a captured German U-boat captain to lunch at his favorite London restaurant and attempt to become friendly in an effort to pick up some scraps of information not yet known to British Naval Intelligence. During one meal, the waiter overheard Mr. Fleming and his guest talking in German about shipping, so the waiter called Scotland Yard. Mr. Fleming and his guest were arrested, and it was some time before Mr. Fleming could convince Scotland Yard that he was not a German spy.[133]

• During an oral test in Divinity, Oxford College, Oscar Wilde was asked to translate out loud a passage from the Greek New Testament. The passage described Christ's Passion and Mr. Wilde translated quickly and fluently. After a number of verses, the Chairman of the Examination Committee told him he could stop, but Mr. Wilde said that he wanted to continue, saying, "Oh, do let me go on. I want to see how it finishes."[134]

• Mark Twain believed that vigorous cussing was one of the greatest joys of life; unfortunately, his wife, Livy, disagreed. One morning, Mr. Twain cut himself while shaving, so he vigorously shouted a long stream of cuss words. Livy, in an attempt to shock him, calmly repeated each word he had said. Mr. Twain smiled at his wife, then said, "You know the words, dear Livy, but you don't know the tune."[135]

• In the first half of the 20th century, John Kieran, a *New York Times* sports columnist, was invited to a forum at an Ivy League university, where some of the students criticized Mr. Kieran's school, Fordham, because it provided its graduates with what they considered a less-than-ideal classical education. Mr. Kieran responded by rising and speaking in defense of Fordham — in Latin.[136]

• Mark Twain wrote in *Innocents Abroad* that when he was in Paris, he fell into the trap of thinking that no one around him could speak English. He told a friend, "Dan, just look at this girl, how beautiful she is!" The "girl" turned to him and said, "I thank you more for the evident sincerity of the compliment, sir, than for the extraordinary publicity you have given to it!"[137]

• Investigative reporter I.F. Stone was very interested in studying the Greek and Latin classics in the original languages. Once he was asked whether he would be able to communicate with Pericles, if the ancient Greek political leader should miraculously come back. "Sure," Mr. Stone replied, "if he spoke Yiddish."[138]

• As a child growing up in Edwight, West Virginia, Mary Carter Smith used to compete in cussing contests. Because she was so good with language, she always won. As an adult, she put her love of language to a much more socially acceptable use as an African-American *griot* (storyteller).[139]

• While in the apartment of poet and Latinist A.E. Housman, Cyril Clemens picked up a copy of an edition of the Roman poet Manilius. When he did so, several pages from the back of the book fell to the floor — obviously, Mr. Housman had made much use of this book.[140]

• Dr. Samuel Johnson, the author of the first comprehensive English dictionary and thus a man who knew the definitions of words, apparently had bad personal hygiene habits. Once a woman told him, "You smell." Dr. Johnson replied, "You smell; I stink."[141]

• Author Mordecai Richler used to tell a story about being in Barcelona in 1951, where he saw a Joel McCrea western movie that had been dubbed. In the movie, Mr. McCrea moseyed up to a bar in a Tombstone saloon and ordered, "*Uno cognac, por favor.*"[142]

Letters

• Openly gay writer Dan Woog receives his share of hate mail; however, he once received a letter that stated, in its entirety, "Dear Dan, I apologize." He has no idea who wrote the letter or what they were apologizing for, but the letter got him thinking about apologies that he wishes other people would make. For example, he wishes that Dick Armey would apologize to fellow politician Barney Frank for calling him "Barney Fag." Such apologies do not occur often in real life, so Mr. Woog decided to write them himself. They appear in his book *Dear Dan ... Apologies From an Imperfect World.*[143]

• Maurice Sendak, author/illustrator of *Where the Wild Things Are* and *In the Night Kitchen*, likes to receive letters from children because they are so honest. He says that when a child likes a book, the child will write something like, "I love your book. Thank you. I want to marry you when I grow up," but if a child doesn't like a book, the child will write something like, "Dear Mr. Sendak: I hate your book. Hope you die soon. Cordially."[144]

• Harold Ross received a letter from a writer who used very fancy stationery that included not only his name and address, but also quotations from critics. Before answering the letter, Mr. Ross had his own fancy stationery created which included this quotation by critic Franklin Pierce Adams: "Among those present was Harold Ross."[145]

• R.L. Stine, author of the *Goosebumps* and *Fear Street* series, receives many letters from his young fans. One of his favorite letters says, "Dear R.L. Stine, I've read forty of your books — and I think they're really boring!"[146]

Marriage

• Lesbian humorist Ellen Orleans has lots of gay men as friends. One day, before gay marriage was legalized, she was having so much fun hanging out with a gay man that one of her friends said that they ought to get married. The thought occurred to Ms. Orleans that she and the gay man could legally get married — although she and her girlfriend couldn't. "Whoa," she said. "He and I actually could." Her friend thought a moment, then said, "Yes, it's legal. Perverse, but legal."[147]

• A little girl reading a Hans Christian Andersen storybook asked satirist George Ade, "Does m-i-r-a-g-e spell marriage?" Mr. Ade answered, "Yes."[148]

CHAPTER 4: From Media to Practical Jokes

Media

• Gene Fowler was the first managing editor of the *New York Mirror*, which was owned by William Randolph Hearst. Before the newspaper began publication, Mr. Hearst ordered Mr. Fowler to create a dummy newspaper that could be run through the presses to make sure the presses were all right. Following orders, Mr. Fowler sat down and wrote an entire newspaper — but every article he wrote for the newspaper was about Mr. Hearst's sex life, including "oddities." When the newspaper had been printed, Mr. Fowler called up Mr. Hearst and reported that the presses were working fine, but after Mr. Fowler had departed for the day, Mr. Hearst decided that he would like to see a copy of the dummy newspaper for himself, so he called the newspaper office and ordered a copy sent to him. When Mr. Fowler returned and discovered that a copy of the newspaper had been sent to Mr. Hearst, he thought that he would very quickly be fired. However, Mr. Hearst merely sent him a telegram: "DEAR GENE FOWLER. FOUND YOUR FIRST ISSUE OF THE 'MIRROR' VERY LIVELY, VERY ENTERTAINING. HOPE SUCCEEDING ISSUES WILL BE A LITTLE MORE CAREFUL ABOUT LIBEL. GOOD LUCK, WILLIAM RANDOLPH HEARST."[149]

• In the early days of the 20th century, the editor of a small-town newspaper in Indiana wanted to delay the afternoon edition of the paper until he received word of who had won the Indianapolis 500. In those days, the fastest form of communication was the telegraph, so the editor made arrangements for him to be telegraphed the name of the winner. Being nervous about holding up the afternoon edition of the newspaper, the editor telegraphed his correspondent, reminding him that the afternoon edition was being held up. The correspondent telegraphed back, "WILL OVERHEAD WINNER." In telegram language, this meant that the correspondent would send the name of the winner by telegram when it was available. Unfortunately, the editor didn't realize that, and the afternoon edition of the newspaper appeared with the headline "Will Overhead Wins Race" with a short article about a racer named Will Overhead coming out of nowhere to win the Indianapolis 500.[150]

• As an early 20th-century newspaperman, Ben Hecht was a picture chaser. Camera equipment back then was difficult to lug around, and so picture chasers would sneak into houses and steal photographs of people in the news so they could print them in their newspaper. Often, Mr. Hecht would pretend to be a census taker or a bill collector to get into a house so he could steal a photograph from a mantel or off a wall. However, the champion picture chaser in Chicago was a man by the name of Leroy T. Benzinger. He would knock on a door, and when the lady of the house answered, he would take out his glass eye. After the lady of the house had fainted, he would walk into her house and steal the photograph his newspaper needed.[151]

• Anne Royall, a feminist and muckraker, knew how to get an interview. President John Quincy Adams did not want to give her an interview, so she followed him. He went to the Potomac River, took off his clothes, then went swimming. Ms. Royall came out of her hiding spot, sat down on his clothes, and declined to leave until after he had answered all her questions. As a muckraker, she made Francis Scott Key so angry that he, Joseph Gales (publisher of the *Washington Intelligencer*), and John Eaton (Secretary of War under President Andrew Jackson) had her arrested as a common scold. In court, she was found guilty of the charge, but the judge declined to give her the prescribed punishment — being dipped on a dunking stool. Instead, he fined her $10.[152]

• As a young reporter in Chicago, Charles MacArthur interviewed Spanish novelist Vincente Blasco Ibáñez, author of *Blood and Sand* (which was later made into a movie starring Rudolph Valentino), for the *Tribune*. Mr. MacArthur interviewed the celebrated author in his hotel room, where Mr. Blasco Ibáñez was lounging in bed. Immediately, Mr. Blasco Ibáñez launched into vociferous criticism of all things Chicagoan. The next day, Mr. MacArthur's story appeared on the front page of the *Tribune*. He had written a few words about the celebrated author's tirade against Chicago, but most of the article's 1,000 words were devoted to a description of Mr. Blasco Ibáñez' toes, which had been clearly visible as he lay in bed.[153]

• David F. Day and Gerald Letcher went West together in 1878. Soon, they decided to start a newspaper in Ouray, Colorado. Thinking about a name for the newspaper, Mr. Day said that the name must be solid and honest — like the famous prizefighter Bill Muldoon. Therefore, they named the newspaper *The Solid Muldoon*. Soon, the newspaper was one of the most widely read in the West, largely because of the crusading spirit of Mr. Day, who stood up for the rights of the people. Although Mr. Day faced as many as 47 libel suits at one time, none of the people suing him for slander ever received as much as a penny.[154]

• People have been suspicious of the media for decades. When Hugh Troy worked at a security job in Washington D.C., he was required to write a memo reporting in detail on every conversation he had with a member of the media. Since he lived next door to a newspaper publisher, Mr. Troy was greatly annoyed by this rule. Finally, he sent in a memo detailing a conversation with a representative of the *Washington Post* — his paperboy. The rule was terminated.[155]

• Many professional writers find writing difficult and are chronically late with copy that is due at magazines. Often, a magazine editor would call humorist Robert Benchley, who frequently made use of messenger boys, with an inquiry about the whereabouts of copy that was due the week before. Mr. Benchley used to drive editors mad with the gentle comment, "My goodness, hasn't that boy got there yet?"[156]

• When Maury Maverick, Jr., served in the Texas House of Representatives in the 1950s, he introduced a bill that would raise the amount of money spent on food in Texas mental institutions from 75 cents to $1.10 per patient — thus allowing the patients to eat three meals a day. The headline about the bill in the *Dallas Morning News* the next day said, "Liberals Run Amok."[157]

• Humorous poet Oliver Herford's wife came up with the idea to start a weekly publication titled *Dreamland*, which would publish contributors' work only if the author could prove that it had been rejected by at least three major publishing houses. Mr. Herford liked the idea, and they started the weekly.[158]

• A Washington newspaper printed a headline with a typo: "CHURCHILL IN BED WITH SLIGHT COED." President Franklin D. Roosevelt sent Prime Minister Winston Churchill several copies of the newspaper.[159]

Money

• Long ago, a friend of Peg Bracken's gave a large business dinner at a San Francisco hotel. Service was mediocre, and the dinner did not have the fresh asparagus he had ordered but instead had canned peas. When it was time to tip, the friend took $20 out of his pocket — a little over 11 percent instead of the customary 15 percent for very good (not mediocre) service. The waiter refused to take the $20, saying, "I'm sorry, sir, but we get 15 percent." The friend said, "As you know, this is a voluntary act on my act. And you say it isn't enough?" The waiter said, "No, it's not enough." So the friend put the $20 back in his pocket and left.[160]

• Mark Twain dedicated his first book — *The Celebrated Jumping Frog of Calaveras County, and Other Sketches* — to "John Smith" because he had heard that people always buy a copy of any book that is dedicated to them. Mr. Twain wrote, "It is said that the man to whom a volume is dedicated, always buys a copy. If this prove true in the present instance, a princely affluence is about to burst upon the author."[161]

• During a literary discussion in which lesbian author Valerie Taylor was participating, this question came up: "What is the function of the novel?" Jim, Ms. Taylor's son, was listening, and he responded, "The function of the novel is to pay the rent." Later, Ms. Taylor discovered that Thomas Hardy had said the same thing in a preface to one of his novels, so she bought a copy of the novel as a gift for her son.[162]

• While in Paris, author Mordecai Richler was taken advantage of by several people demanding tips. A doorman removed his bags from a taxi, carried them to the front door, then extended his hand for a tip. Another man carried his bags to the registration desk, then extended his hand for a tip. A third man carried his bags to his hotel room, then extended his hand for a tip.[163]

• When horror writer Stephen King leaves his house to buy a loaf of bread, he sometimes gets so caught up in creating a plot for a novel that he forgets to buy the bread. After coming home, he tells his wife that he has an idea for a novel that will make them $2 million. She usually replies, "Steve, I'm delighted, but we still need a loaf of bread."[164]

• Noël Coward was very broke when he received an offer of $500 to write a short story using the plot of one of his plays. Mr. Coward was happy to receive the money and later said, "I reflected gleefully that for $500 I would gladly consider turning *War and Peace* into a music-hall sketch."[165]

• Playwright Richard Brinsley Sheridan was always in debt. One day, a creditor asked him to at least pay the interest on a debt. Mr. Sheridan replied, "My dear fellow, it is not in my interest to pay the principle or in my principle to pay the interest."[166]

Mothers

• When author Joel Perry was nine years old, he was victimized by a bully who lived next door. The bully pretended to be his friend and threw a baseball to Joel so he could hit it, but Joel was not an athlete and kept missing the ball, giving the bully an excuse to taunt him. Finally, the bully came up close and personal, screaming at him, "You are so stupid! How can you be such a fat, stupid sissy, you crybaby retard!" Joel swung the bat and connected — with the bully's head. The bully's mother came running, grabbed Joel, took him to his home, and complained to his mother, who said, "I'll handle this" and shut the door. After shutting the door, his mother said to him, "I saw the whole thing. What the hell took you so long?" As a special treat, she bought him ice cream, then took him to the park to feed the ducks.[167]

• Sir Arthur Conan Doyle (the creator of Sherlock Holmes) and his wife were believers in spiritualism; escape artist Harry Houdini was not. Nevertheless, they all became friends. One evening, Lady Conan Doyle held a séance and attempted to contact Houdini's deceased mother. She fell into a trance and wrote down a message for Houdini from his mother, then she came out of the trance. The Conan Doyles regarded the séance as a complete success; however, Houdini did not. The message Lady Doyle had written was in English — a language his Yiddish-speaking mother did not know.[168]

• Irving Wallace's mother made an excellent strudel — baked dough with a filling of nuts, fruits, and other goodies. One day, she had a strudel ready to be rolled up and baked when the telephone rang. As she talked on the telephone, occasionally she would reach out, grab a few nuts, fruits, or other goodies, then eat them as she talked. Finally, she hung up the telephone and told young Irving, "Now we're going to roll the strudel and bake it," then she looked at the strudel and realized that she had eaten all the filling. That day, the Wallace family didn't have a strudel.[169]

• Oscar Wilde's mother was decidedly unconventional. Under the name "Speranza," Lady Wilde wrote pro-Irish revolutionary tracts. One day, a friend of hers asked if she could bring a "respectable" friend to one of Lady Wilde's parties, and Lady Wilde replied, "You must never employ that description in this house; only tradespeople are respectable." On another occasion, Oscar invited a fellow student to his home, saying, "I want to introduce you to my mother. We have founded a society for the suppression of virtue."[170]

• Humor writer Erma Bombeck spoke early and often in support of the Equal Rights Amendment, which failed to become law in the 1980s. In doing so, she was criticized by many people, including a politician who said that she should be at home having babies. Ms. Bombeck pointed out that her "babies" — she had adopted a girl and given birth to two boys — were old enough to vote against the politician.[171]

• Lesbian author Kay Wolff adopted a couple of children in Colombia and began attending PTA meetings and taking her children to soccer practice. One day, the soccer coach patted her on the back and said, "We know how hard it is for a single mother." She replied, "I am not a single mother. I am a lesbian."[172]

• Lesbian author Gail Sausser's coming out to her mother was non-traumatic, as her mother simply said, "I know." Gail was surprised and asked, "How could you know?" Her mother replied, "I watched you grow up."[173]

Music

• Michael Thomas Ford, author of *That's* Mr. Faggot *to You*, once attended a gay pride rally in New York in which speaker after speaker got up and spoke about the gains that had been made by gays and lesbians. He cheered and pumped his fist, but still felt guilty for being slightly bored. After all, he thought, this could be any rally for any group. There wasn't anything at the rally that set gays and lesbians off as being different — and isn't being different part of what's good about being gay? Just then, the loudspeakers poured forth Gloria Gaynor's "I Will Survive," and 7,000 gays and lesbians jumped to their feet and started dancing. Mr. Ford joyfully writes, "It was a moment that could only happen when 7,000 queers stood up and reminded themselves that it's a lot more fun to be different, even if it costs us something."[174]

• After retiring from opera, Geraldine Farrar began giving music concerts. At one midwestern college, a student newspaper reporter spoke to her, explaining that he had a problem. He had been asked to write a review of her concert, but the only thing he knew enough to write about was football. Therefore, he asked that she write her own review. She did so, giving only modest praise to herself, but heaping praise upon her artistic colleagues. One colleague was especially pleased by the review, and he used to quote it in advertisements in trade papers. Ms. Farrar never told him who had really written the review.[175]

• On the 1922 trip, E.B. White took along a one-stringed instrument he had created from a stick and a cigar box — and which he played with a worn violin bow. Apparently, Mr. White was good with the instrument; he once played a flawless "Wearing of the Green" for an Irish gas station attendant in return for a tank of gas.[176]

Names

• When Ian Fleming was looking for a simple, but solid, name for a British spy character in his novels, he looked over his book collection and found the perfect name in the ornithologist author of *Birds of the West Indies*: James Bond. Mr. Fleming met Mr. Bond after his books had made the name "James Bond" famous. Fortunately, Mr. Bond regarded it all as great fun.[177]

• Each year, the members of the Science Fiction Writers of America give the Nebula Award. Unfortunately, the Nebula Award that Isaac Asimov won in 1976 for Best Novelette reveals a problem that Mr. Asimov was faced with throughout his career — people find his name difficult to spell. The notation on the Nebula Award says that its winner is ISAAC ASMIMOV.[178]

• In the 1930s, writer Alice Mary Norton had her name legally changed to Andre Norton because at that time men were able more easily than women to sell their writing. Ms. Norton became the famous author of such fantasies as *Witch World* and *Star Gate*.[179]

Nobel Prizes

• The Nobel Prizes are awarded by a committee of 11 Swedish men. For a prize to be given, the 11 men have to vote unanimously; otherwise, no prize is given in that category in that year. This means that one or two men on the committee can keep certain nominees from winning. In 1976, Saul Bellow won the Nobel Prize for Literature. Previously, he had been on the short list of writers considered for the award, but two men on the selection committee had opposed his winning. However, the two men died, and Mr. Bellow won the award. When he heard the inside story of how he had been chosen for the award, Mr. Bellow said, "Oh, you mean it only took two men to die for me to get the Nobel Prize!"[180]

• Princess Grace of Monaco sent John Steinbeck a congratulatory letter when he won the Nobel Prize in Literature in 1962, so Mr. Steinbeck asked his wife to look up the proper way to address an envelope to a princess so he could reply with the proper etiquette. Mrs. Steinbeck did so, then asked if he knew the proper way to begin the letter. "Sure," said Mr. Steinbeck. "I've already written it: 'Princess Grace, honey — .'"[181]

• Dorothy Parker taught at Los Angeles State College, where she discovered that the students were "narrow." She had them read John Steinbeck's *Grapes of Wrath*, but the students disliked the book, saying it was dirty. However, when Mr. Steinbeck won the Nobel Prize for Literature, the students' attitudes changed. According to Mrs. Parker, "After that, they behaved as if they had given it to him."[182]

Old Age

• In his old age, James M. Barrie, the author of *Peter Pan*, was forced to write with his left hand instead of his right. His secretary, Lady Cynthia Asquith (who got her job partly because she didn't know how to type — Mr. Barrie disliked the sound of a typewriter), later wrote, "I remember his announcing this change quite formally, as though in dismissing his right hand he were giving notice to a servant of many years faithful service."[183]

• While visiting China, African-American author Alice Walker met the great Chinese woman writer Ding Ling, who had been imprisoned for opposing the subjection of women. Although Ding Ling was still writing at age 80, she wished that she could have back the time she had lost while being persecuted. She told Ms. Walker, "Oh, to be 67 again!"[184]

Plays

• Actor Robert Morley enjoyed changing the dialogue of the plays he appeared in, including Peter Ustinov's *Halfway Up the Tree*. When Mr. Ustinov saw the play, he told Mr. Morley that it was "very funny." Mr. Morley said, "That's a relief, Peter. By this time I'm usually not talking to the author." Mr. Ustinov replied, "What? Not even talking to yourself?" When Mr. Morley left the play and was replaced by actor Jimmy Edwards, Mr. Ustinov said, "I think Jimmy Edwards will be great. My only concern is what he will do to Bob Morley's script."[185]

• It's easy to believe that Alexander Woollcott was the real-life inspiration for Sheridan Whiteside, the very unpleasant guest in George S. Kaufman and Moss Hart's comic play *The Man Who Came to Dinner*. After all, Mr. Woollcott once wrote in Mr. Hart's guest book: "This is to certify that on my first visit to Moss Hart's house I had one of the most unpleasant times I ever spent."[186]

• Changes are frequently made in the scripts of plays before they open on Broadway. Zero Mostel was in the play *Beggar's Holiday* when the director said, "Okay, let's go back to the original script, before the changes." Unfortunately, nobody any longer had the original script — not the composer, not the director, not even the author.[187]

• When they were teenagers, Noël Coward and Collie Knox attended at a party at which a playwright walked around with his nose stuck up in the air. Mr. Coward said, "One day, I shall write a play. It will be a success, but I shall try not to look like that. Come, let's have an ice cream."[188]

• Lesbian writer Hollie Hughes' first play was *The Well of Horniness*, with Garnet McClit as the main character. One of the stage directions in the play is this: "Feel free to go too far; it's the only way to go in this play."[189]

Poetry and Poets

• Langston Hughes wrote poetry in what time he could and worked in a restaurant to make money. One day, while working at the restaurant, he discovered that the famous poet Vachel Lindsay was dining there. Therefore, he put some of his poems next to Mr. Lindsay's dinner plate, where the famous poet would be sure to see them. Mr. Lindsay saw the poems, read them, and liked what he read. That night, he gave a poetry reading at which he read his own poems — and some poems by Mr. Hughes. Newspapers covered the poetry reading, and Mr. Hughes became known as an up-and-coming African-American poet.[190]

• The literary career of poet Dave Smith took a giant leap forward in 1975, when *The New Yorker* began to print his poetry. Suddenly, his work was in demand. Regarding the new eagerness of literary journals to print his poems, he said, "A year ago [they] were sending my things back with straight rejection slips. I'm a little baffled by it all. I can't believe I've gotten so much better in the last year and attribute it to the power of publishing in high visibility places." His work did get better — a couple of his volumes of poetry have been finalists for the Pulitzer Prize.[191]

• Oscar Wilde greatly respected American poet Walt Whitman and made sure to meet him during his lecture tour through America. At the meeting, the two poets got along well, and Mr. Whitman served his guest elderberry wine. Later, a friend of Mr. Wilde's, knowing his epicurean tastes, said that it must have been difficult for him to drink the elderberry wine. Mr. Wilde replied, "If it had been vinegar, I should have drunk it all the same."[192]

• Scottish poet Robert Burns attended church in Dumfries, where the minister was fiercely denouncing sinners. Mr. Burns noticed a young woman, Miss Ainslie, looking through her Bible, trying to find the passage the preacher was referring to. Mr. Burns scribbled a few verses, then handed them to her:

"Fair Maid, you need not take the hint,

"Nor idle texts pursue;

"'Twas guilty sinners that he meant,

"Not angels — such as you!"[193]

• Emily Dickinson became a renowned American poet even though her father and her church were against reading. Her father believed that books "joggle the mind," and the Congregational Church thought that reading was bad for young people. Nevertheless, Ms. Dickinson — always a nonconformist — started a Shakespeare Club in which members read a book and then gathered together and discussed it.[194]

• When she was seven years old, P.L. Travers, the author of *Mary Poppins*, wrote poetry, which she showed to her father, who was not impressed and who told her, "Hardly W.B. Yeats." Ms. Travers points out, "It would have been hard even for Yeats to be W.B. Yeats at the age of seven!"[195]

Practical Jokes

• David F. Day was the editor of a Democratic paper in Colorado in the late 1800s and supported the silver standard. Once, he was visited by Francis E. Leupp, a journalist who was a Republican and who supported the gold standard. In addition to being a newspaper editor, Mr. Day was also busy as the Indian Agent for the Southern Ute Indians. Because he was so busy, Mr. Day allowed Mr. Leupp to write the editorial for the week of his visit and ordered his newspaper to print whatever Mr. Leupp wrote. Mr. Leupp took advantage of Mr.

Day's generosity by writing "A Confession Wrung from Conscience," an editorial piece ostensibly written by Mr. Day, but which totally reversed Mr. Day's position, arguing in favor of the gold standard instead of the silver standard. Because Mr. Day lived in a silver-mining area where arguing in favor of the gold standard was both unpopular and likely to be dangerous, he was forced to hide his family until he could explain the cruel practical joke in the next week's edition of his newspaper.[196]

• Mark Twain was addicted to practical jokes — especially when they were jokes he played on other people. One day, when he was looking out the window of an editor's office on the third floor of a building, he noticed a friend of his standing immediately below. Unfortunately for his friend, Mr. Twain had just been made the recipient of the gift of a watermelon by the editor. You can guess what happened to the friend and the watermelon. Still, Mr. Twain reflected, the friend came out ahead because the practical joke spoiled the watermelon, making it unsuitable for eating.[197]

• James Thurber was ordered to court with a summons intended for John Thurber, his brother. Sitting in the witness seat, Mr. Thurber said that he didn't have his birth certificate, but he did have a driver license, a couple of letters, and a few bills, all of which bore the name James Thurber. The court was convinced that James Thurber was not John Thurber — until humorist Robert Benchley walked into court, looked straight at James Thurber, and said, "How are you, John?"[198]

• Many authors write witty and/or sentimental inscriptions in their books. Humorist Frank Sullivan wrote this inscription to Marise Campbell: "To dear Marise, without whose sympathetic help the undersigned would not have written this book," then signed his name and the date. He wrote this inscription in a 1929 Staten Island telephone directory.[199]

CHAPTER 5: From Prejudice to Work

Prejudice

• Playwright Lorraine Hansberry, author of the play *A Raisin in the Sun*, was born into a financially well-off family. Her father was a real estate agent in Chicago, and he was determined to challenge the legal segregation that kept blacks and whites in their own separate neighborhoods. Therefore, he bought a house in a white neighborhood and moved his family into it. As he expected, the city of Chicago ordered him to move out, and he responded with a lawsuit. In addition, because he expected trouble from his racist white neighbors, he made sure that a bodyguard protected his family when he was away from home, attending to the lawsuit. (Her parents told young Lorraine that the bodyguard was a friend.) At one point, several of their white neighbors gathered together into a mob, and someone threw a chunk of concrete into the Hansberrys' front window, shattering glass everywhere and narrowly missing Lorraine. For a while, Lorraine's mother stayed up late at night, patrolling her house with a loaded gun in her hands. During the tension, friends stopped by frequently and African-American cab drivers drove slowly past the house, checking to make sure that everything was okay. Eventually, the United States Supreme Court ruled in the Hansberrys' favor, thus establishing that people could not be kept out of a particular neighborhood because of their race.[200]

• Near Christmas, at her school in Youngstown, Ohio, eight-year-old Mary Carter Smith waited eagerly to give her teacher a gift. When the time arrived, each of the children lined up and presented the teacher with a gift. The teacher smiled at the children and accepted their gifts, with one exception. When Mary gave her teacher her gift — a white handkerchief with pink edging — the teacher did not smile, but lifted the handkerchief up by the corner, dropped it into a wastebasket, then looked over Mary's shoulder and smiled at the next child in line. At home, Mary cried, told her grandmother what had happened, and asked, "Why did she do that to me?" Her grandmother explained, "Child, you are colored, and that makes a big difference to some people." Fortunately, good teachers also worked in Youngstown. A substitute teacher named Mrs. Showalter told the class about George Washington Carver and Booker T. Washington. As an adult, Ms. Smith recalled, "That was the first time I had heard of anyone my color doing anything worthwhile." Another teacher, Miss Gilbert, told her that she would grow up to be Somebody. Ms. Smith did become Somebody — she became a famous *griot* (storyteller).[201]

• African-American woman writer Ida B. Wells wrote passionately about how blacks were treated in racist America. While teaching in the public schools, she wrote weekly articles for *The Living Way*, but when white politicians learned that she was writing the articles, they made sure that she was fired from her teaching job. Because of this, she bought a newspaper, the *Memphis Free Speech*, and continued to write against injustices, such as when three black businessmen were lynched when they opened a grocery store in competition with a white businessman. A mob destroyed the offices of the *Memphis Free Speech*, and she moved on to New York, where she bought a partial interest in a newspaper and wrote against racism.[202]

• In 1961, Haki R. Madhubuti joined the United States Army. At boot camp, there were 197 white men — and only three African-American men. Stepping off the bus, Mr. Madhubuti carried a copy of *Here I Stand*, by the African-American singer, actor, and civil rights activist Paul Robeson. The drill sergeant seized the book, said something racist, tore the pages out of the book, and gave a page to each new recruit — with orders to use it as toilet paper. Today, Mr. Madhubuti is a famous African-American poet.[203]

• Before World War II, Liz Carpenter, author of *Getting Better All the Time* and *Ruffles and Flourishes*, ran for vice president of the student body of the University of Texas — and was the first woman to be so elected. Her campaign posters said, "If you would vote against me for vice-president of the student body solely because I am a woman, you are a son of a ...."[204]

• In 1951, environmentalist Rachel Carson published her best-selling book *The Sea Around Us*. She received a number of fan letters, including some from sexists. One man wrote his letter to Miss Rachel Carson, which was correct, but then he began his letter with "Dear Sir," explaining that he had always felt that men were intellectually superior to women.[205]

• Investigative reporter I.F. Stone was not welcome at the National Press Club after 1941 because he had brought a black judge as his guest for lunch. He tried to apply for readmission in 1956, but he could not find enough journalists to sponsor his application. Finally, he was readmitted in 1981, 40 years after having a black judge as his guest for lunch.[206]

• American author Laura Z. Hobson (nee Zametkin) was proud of her Jewish heritage. At a dinner party, someone said, "Some of my best friends are Jews." Ms. Hobson spoke up: "Some of mine are, too — including my father and mother."[207]

• As one of the few African-American students at Harvard in the 1890s, W.E.B. Du Bois faced prejudice. At a social function, a young woman insisted that because of his race, he must be a waiter — he couldn't be a guest.[208]

Problem-Solving

• As a young man during World War II, journalist Meyer Berger wanted to enlist in the Army but he was unable to because of his poor eyesight. Fortunately, when Mr. Berger attempted a second time to enlist, an understanding officer told him to wait for five minutes in the room where the eye chart was located. During those five minutes, Mr. Berger memorized the eye chart. Years later, he could still recite the chart horizontally, vertically, forwards, and backwards. In the Army, he had to keep his poor eyesight a secret until he was shipped overseas, so he was put in a regimental band with orders to hold a French horn to his lips — and not attempt to play it. While stationed overseas, his fellow soldiers put what eyesight Mr. Berger had to good use — Mr. Berger wrote love letters for them.[209]

• When Jerry Spinelli, author of the Newbery Medal-winning *Maniac Magee*, attended his ninth-grade prom, the girls were angry because they were not allowed to wear strapless gowns. Not content with merely being angry, the girls also took action. Many of the straps worn to the prom that evening were flimsy — one "strap" consisted of a single piece of thread. Another girl's "straps" were actually lines painted with eyeliner. Of course, some girls wore real straps — but they carried scissors in their purses. By the last dance, every girl had bare shoulders.[210]

• M.E. Kerr, one of the pseudonyms of Marijane Meaker, was the author of such young people's books as *Dinky Hocker Shoots Smack*. She enjoyed frequent visits by teenagers in her neighborhood, but she devised a means to get privacy when she needed it. Whenever she wanted to be alone, she hung a stuffed rabbit on her door. When the neighborhood teenagers saw the stuffed rabbit, they didn't visit.[211]

• Nicholasa Mohr worked as a professional artist before she began to write such children's books as *Nilda*. As a child, she lived in a rough neighborhood, and to keep the tough kids from beating her up, she offered to draw their portraits. Ms. Mohr says, "I would make sure they looked really good, almost like movie stars!"[212]

• The door to Jane Austen's sitting room creaked. Why didn't Ms. Austen have it oiled? It gave her warning that visitors were coming, so she was able to hide her writing before her visitors came into the room.[213]

Public Speaking

• On March 28, 1963, Dr. Martin Luther King, Jr., gave his famous March on Washington Address — the one in which he said, "I have a dream." Among the people present that day was novelist Alice Walker, who later wrote the Pulitzer Prize-winning *The Color Purple*. On the day of Dr. King's speech, Ms. Walker climbed a tree in the national capitol — from her perch, she saw very little, but she heard everything.[214]

• Maxine Hong Kingston won the National Book Critics Circle Award for nonfiction with her 1976 book, *The Woman Warrior*. When she gave a speech at the awards ceremony, she was unable to see over the podium because she is only four feet, nine inches tall. Therefore, she bent sideways around the podium and gave her acceptance speech.[215]

Research

• While doing research for her children's book *A Snake's Body*, Joanna Cole met in her home with a snake expert from the New York City Museum of Natural History. He had brought a snakeskin for her to look at, but when he showed it to Ms. Cole, her pet dog, Taffy, jumped in the air and grabbed it. Taffy then disappeared under a bed, where she apparently ate the snakeskin. The snake expert told Ms. Cole, "Don't worry. We have plenty of them back at the lab."[216]

• Peter Ustinov says that being famous is a handicap when it comes to doing first-hand research. For example, he can't go into a brothel in Hamburg, Germany, to do research for a thriller because people ask him for his autograph.[217]

Revenge

• When the parents of author Michael Thomas Ford divorced after a long marriage, his mother — who had run away with another man — sent his father a long list of items that she said she would come by and pick up. She also included a much shorter list of items that she would allow him to keep. After receiving the letter. Mr. Ford's father spent a lot of time in the horse barn. Soon, Mr. Ford's mother came by and loaded up a huge U-Haul truck with stuff she and her husband had accumulated together during 35 years of marriage, and she also loaded ten heavy boxes labeled "Dishes" and "Garden Stuff," leaving behind a piano she didn't have room for. After she had left, Mr. Ford's father had a big smile on his face, and Mr. Ford asked him why. His father replied, "Did you see those big cardboard boxes? The ones marked 'Dishes' and 'Garden Stuff'? I put those there. They were filled with bags of horse sh*t taken from the barn."[218]

• The ancient Greek poet Ibykos (who lived in the 6th century B.C.E.) was said to have been murdered by robbers. Before dying, he exclaimed to the robbers that some birds — cranes — nearby would be his avengers. The robbers laughed at him and murdered him anyway. When the robbers entered a city later, one of the robbers saw some cranes and shouted, "Look — the avengers of Ibykos." This aroused the curiosity of the citizens of the city, who — after investigating and discovering that the robbers had murdered Ibykos — put the robbers to death.[219]

Sales

• Valerie Taylor was one of the first people to write positive lesbian fiction. She remembers the first time she saw someone buying one of her novels. She felt like rushing up to him, shaking his hand, and thanking him, but managed to restrain herself.[220]

• After James M. Barrie, author of *Peter Pan*, wrote his first book, *Better Dead*, and paid a publisher to print it, he used to hang around newsstands, hoping to see someone buy a copy.[221]

Sex

• Screenwriter Gene Fowler was tending the lawn of his California home when a car drove up to him and stopped, then the driver asked about a glamorous, sexy movie star, "Does Lana Turner live here?" Mr. Fowler looked up and answered, "If Lana Turner lived here, do you think I would be outdoors?"[222]

• While Dorothy Parker was on her honeymoon, editor Harold Ross sent her a telegram asking her if she had finished an article she was writing for *The New Yorker*. She replied with this telegram: "TOO F*CKING BUSY, AND VICE VERSA."[223]

Sports

• When he was a young boy, young people's book author Walter Dean Myers went with some other boys to a church gym, where they hoped to play full-court basketball. They were disappointed when they found half of the court occupied by girls who danced, then stretched. The boys made what they thought were appropriately disgusted comments, and the girls made a deal with them. If the boys could do the stretching exercises that the girls were doing, the girls would leave and allow the boys to play full-court basketball, but if the boys could not do the stretching exercises, then they had to perform the dance routine with them. The boys accepted the offer, but they quickly discovered that none of them were limber enough to do the stretching exercises that the girls were doing. The girls made the boys live up to the deal they had made — the boys had to perform the dance routine with them.[224]

• Sports writers sometimes lead interesting lives. Back when figure skater Katarina Witt was competing internationally for East Germany, many people believed that the East German athletes were using steroids. (In fact, some were.) However, at a press conference, Ms. Witt denied ever using steroids. She leaned forward, then told the sports writers, "Look at these boobs! If I were on steroids, would I have boobs like this?"[225]

Thanksgiving

• For a party, gay author Joel Perry ordered a turkey to be prepared by HoneyBaked. Unfortunately, when he arrived with his reservation number to pick up the turkey, he was informed that it had already been sold. One other turkey was on display, so he asked if he could buy it, but the salesperson informed him that someone else was buying it. A gay man expecting 20 people for dinner is not to be trifled with, so Mr. Perry jumped over the counter, grabbed the turkey, threw down $50, and then dashed out of the store.[226]

Titles

• Children's book author Lois Lowry plays a game with children and other people, a game with no wrong answers. The game is played when she and others are looking at a scene, and someone asks, "What book does this scene remind you of?" For a meadow scene, the answers may range from *Gone With the Wind* to *Wind in the Willows* to *Where the Wild Things Are*. All of these answers are right. Usually, the answers differ considerably, but on one occasion everyone came up with the same book title. Watching a 15-month-old boy play with his food in a high chair, everyone answered, *James and the Giant Peach*.[227]

• Cranston Toller was and is a controversial, outspoken figure skater and artist. When Mr. Toller wrote *Zero Tollerance*, his autobiography, an editor suggested that he subtitle it *Chronicles of a Misspent Life*. Mr. Toller would have none of that, saying, "How dare you? My life has not been misspent. My life has been textured."[228]

• Gail Godwin wrote a novel titled *The Good Husband*. She sent her assistant to copy some of the pages from the manuscript, and her assistant reported that while she was copying the pages, another woman had seen the title and snorted, "Ha! Where? Let me know when you find him."[229]

Tobacco

• Andrew Tobias, a progressive and an anti-smoking activist, was annoyed by a plane flying over his vacation home and displaying the pro-tobacco banner "Newport: Alive with Pleasure," so he hired another plane to display the banner "Larry Tisch Sells Cancer Sticks." (At the time, Larry Tisch controlled the company that manufactures Newport cigarettes.) The next summer, another pro-tobacco plane flew over his vacation home bearing the banner "Parliament: The Perfect Recess." (This sounds like a tobacco advertisement aimed at schoolchildren.) So Mr. Tobias hired another plane to display the banner "Parliament: The PERMANENT Recess." The summer after that, no pro-tobacco plane appeared, so Mr. Tobias hired a final plane to display the banner "Thank You for Not Smoking."[230]

• As you would expect, children's book author Dr. Seuss had a quirky sense of humor. When he decided to quit smoking, he bought a corncob pipe and put radish seeds in its bowl. After boarding a bus, he put the unlit pipe in his mouth, held it there for several minutes, then pulled an eyedropper from his pocket and squirted several drops of water into the bowl. Of course, a woman asked him, "What are you doing?" Dr. Seuss replied, "I'm watering the radishes."[231]

Travel

• While Mark Twain was traveling in Europe (an adventure he wrote about in *Innocents Abroad*), a number of tour guides made his life miserable, so with the help of a few friends, he decided to make the tour guides' lives miserable. For the duration of the trip, Mark Twain and his friends refused to be impressed by anything a tour guide showed them. Once, a tour guide showed them a letter handwritten by Christopher Columbus. One of Mark Twain's friends looked at the letter and complained about the sloppy penmanship, "Why, I have seen boys in America only fourteen years old that could write better than that."[232]

• Meindert DeJong was born in Friesland, a province of the Netherlands, and he had the blond hair of his countrymen. During World War II, having moved to America, he joined the United States Air Force and was stationed in the Chungking area of China. There, his blond hair fascinated the Chinese. Many wanted to touch it — but some women were so frightened by it that they ran away from him. Later, Mr. DeJong became the renowned author of such children's books as *The House of the Sixty Fathers*, a story about a Chinese boy struggling to survive in wartime.[233]

• Basho, the famous writer of haiku, decided to visit a place that was famed for its beautiful flowers. While traveling there, he heard about a peasant girl who was famed for her tender devotion to her parents. Basho visited the peasant girl, and he discovered that her devotion to her parents had not been exaggerated. Basho then gave her all the money he had saved for his trip and returned home, saying, "This year I have seen something better than flowers."[234]

- In 1922, E.B. White and a friend drove across the country in a Model T they named Hotspur (from a character in Shakespeare's *Henry IV, Part 1*), eventually ending up in Seattle, but not before watching the Kentucky Derby. Mr. White lost $5 (approximately $94 in 2024) betting on the race, but recouped his loss by writing a poem about the winner of the race and selling it to the *Louisville Herald*.[235]

- While visiting the cathedral at Milan, Italy, Mark Twain and a friend wished to go aloft. A sacristan told the party "to go up one hundred and eighty-two steps and stop till he came." According to Mr. Twain, "It was not necessary to say stop — we should have done that any how. We were tired by the time we got there."[236]

- Johanna Hurwitz, author of *Busybody Nora*, usually writes in her study, although while traveling, she occasionally writes elsewhere. During an airplane trip, a flight attendant asked her if she wanted a beverage. Ms. Hurwitz looked up from her writing and wondered, "What is this lady doing in my study?"[237]

- James Boswell said about a well-known tourist destination that the pleasure of seeing it wasn't worth even half a guinea. His friend, Samuel Johnson, replied, "But, sir, there is half a guinea's worth of inferiority to other people in not having seen it."[238]

Work

- Jonathan Swift once traveled with a lazy servant. One night, he gave his boots to the lazy servant to clean and shine, but the next morning they were still dirty. When Dean Swift asked for an explanation, the lazy servant said that he had not cleaned them because Dean Swift was going to ride again today, and what was the use of cleaning them if they were just going to get dirty again. Hearing that, Dean Swift told the servant to get ready immediately to continue their journey. The servant protested, "But I haven't eaten breakfast yet!" Dean Swift responded, "What is the use of feeding you breakfast if you are just going to get hungry again?" After that, Dean Swift had his boots cleaned and shined each night, and the servant ate breakfast each morning.[239]

• In *Roughing It*, Mark Twain wrote about working as a common laborer in a quartz mill, where he refined silver ore into silver bricks. After a week of backbreaking labor, he went to his employer and said that although he had come to love the work, he felt that he could not continue working without a raise. The employer countered by saying that he was paying Mr. Twain $10 a week, which he felt was a fair sum, and just how much of a raise did Mr. Twain want? Mark Twain replied that $400,000 a month, and board, was all he could reasonably ask, considering the hard times. Of course, Mr. Twain was then ordered off the premises of the quartz mill.[240]

• Frederick C. Copleston, S.J. wrote a nine-volume history of philosophy, an accomplishment that astonished many people, who suspected that a syndicate of writers was actually behind the books published under the name of Copleston. He once said, "If anyone is curious to know how I managed to write so much, the answer is, I suppose, that I did little else but study, lecture, and write. Being celibate and having for most of my life no administrative post, I was able to devote a large part of each day to literary work. The syndicate idea was a figment of the imagination."[241]

• Children's book author/illustrator David McPhail believes in taking advantage of inspiration when it strikes. He was awaiting some friends whom he had invited to his house when he was struck by inspiration and began writing *Henry Bear's Park*. In the middle of writing the story, he heard a knock at the door. He threw it open, saw his friends, and told them, "I'm in the middle of writing something. Go to the beach and come back in an hour!" An hour later, when they came back, he had finished the story.[242]

• Robert Benchley frequently found it difficult to work at his apartment in the Algonquin — friends were always dropping in to see him, or he was always leaving his apartment to drop in on some of his friends. Once, he wrote the word "The" on a sheet of paper, figuring that it would make a good beginning for an article, then he went out to see some friends. When he returned, he stared for a while at the "The," then added "hell with it," and went out to see some more friends.[243]

• Zora Neale Hurston, author of *Their Eyes were Watching God*, made little money as a writer although she was one of the most celebrated writers of the Harlem Renaissance. At one point, despite being a published writer, she worked as a maid in Florida to make money because she needed money and was accustomed to earn her own way in life. Members of the white family she worked for were greatly surprised one day when they saw a photograph of their maid in a magazine.[244]

• Lois Ehlert did not plan to be a writer/illustrator of children's books, but after taking a class on making homemade books, she needed something to fill the pages of the book she had created. Because she had a vegetable garden, she wrote and illustrated a story that she titled *Growing Vegetable Soup*. The book was published, and suddenly Ms. Ehlert was a writer/illustrator of books for children.[245]

• The worst job author Gary Paulsen ever had was replacing septic tanks while working for a septic tank company. Because he was new at the company, he had the worst job — emptying the sewage from the old tanks. Sometimes, Mr. Paulsen would be shoveling when a homeowner flushed the toilet and unintentionally gave him a shower of sewage — Mr. Paulsen's fellow employees thought this was hilarious.[246]

• As the author of such children's books as *The Two Giants*, Eve Bunting finds that she can write anywhere. Because she didn't have her notebook with her, she once wrote a children's story on the back of a program in the dark while a play was being performed. On another occasion, she felt inspired while traveling but again didn't have her notebook with her, so she wrote the story on a "barf" bag.[247]

• As an author of children's books, Margaret Mahy stays alert in hopes of finding ideas for new books. She once saw this sign in a butcher's shop in her native New Zealand: "Pot-boiling owls." Actually, a letter had fallen off the sign — it was supposed to say, "Pot-boiling Fowls." Someday, she may write a story suggested by this sign.[248]

• As a hard-working professional writer, Isaac Asimov, who wrote or edited over 400 books during his career, began writing at 7:30 a.m. then continued throughout the day, often writing until late at night. He once said, "I *must* write. I look upon everything *but* writing as an interruption."[249]

• Finis Farr worked as a contributing editor at *Time*, where he was very unhappy. One day, he went to a park after lunch and thought how much he dreaded going back to work. Suddenly, he thought, "I've got the answer! Don't go back." Mr. Farr didn't go back.[250]

Appendix A: Bibliography

Adams, Franklin P., et. al. *Percy Hammond: A Symposium in Tribute*. Garden City, NY: Doubleday, Doran & Co., Inc., 1936.

Adams, Joey. *The God Bit*. Boston, MA: G.K. Hall & Co., 1975.

Allen, Everett S. *Famous American Humorous Poets*. New York: Dodd, Mead & Company, 1968.

Aller, Susan Bivin. *J.M. Barrie: The Magic Behind Peter Pan*. Minneapolis, MN: Lerner Publications Company, 1994.

Bailey, Paul, editor. *The Stately Homo: A Celebration of the Life of Quentin Crisp*. London: Bantam Press, 2000.

Barnstone, Willis, translator. *Greek Lyric Poetry*. New York: Schocken Books, 1967.

Benchley, Nathaniel. *Robert Benchley*. New York: McGraw-Hill Book Company, Inc., 1955.

Bernard, André. *Now All We Need is a Title: Famous Book Titles and How They Got That Way*. New York: W.W. Norton & Company, 1995.

Bombeck, Erma. *I Want to Grow Hair, I Want to Grow Up, I Want to Go to Boise*. New York: Harper and Row, Publishers, 1989.

Bracken, Peg. *But I Wouldn't Have Missed It for the World!* New York: Harcourt Brace Jovanovich, Inc., 1973.

Bracken, Peg. *I Didn't Come Here to Argue*. New York: Harcourt, Brace and World, Inc., 1969.

Bredeson, Carmen. *American Writers of the 20th Century*. Springfield, NJ: Enslow Publications, Inc., 1996.

Bronski, Michael, consulting editor. *Outstanding Lives: Profiles of Lesbians and Gay Men*. Foreword by Jewelle L. Gomez; Christa Brelin and Michael J. Tyrkus, editors. Detroit, MI: Visible Ink Press, 1997.

Brown, Michèle and Ann O'Connor. *Hammer and Tongues: A Dictionary of Women's Wit and Humour*. London: J.M. Dent and Sons, Ltd., 1986.

Bryan III, J. *Merry Gentlemen (and One Lady)*. New York: Atheneum, 1985.

Bryce, Ivar. *You Only Live Once: Memories of Ian Fleming*. London: Weidenfeld and Nicolson, 1984.

Bunting, Eve. *Once Upon a Time*. Katonah, New York: Richard C. Owen Publishers, Inc., 1995.

Carpenter, Angelica Shirley, and Jean Shirley. *L. Frank Baum: Royal Historian of Oz*. Minneapolis, MN: Lerner Publications Company, 1992.

Carter, Judy. *The Homo Handbook*. New York: Fireside Books, 1996.

Chappell, Helen. *The Chesapeake Book of the Dead: Tombstones, Epitaphs, Histories, Reflections, and Oddments of the Region.* Baltimore, MD: The Johns Hopkins University Press, 1999.

Charles, Helen White, collector and editor. *Quaker Chuckles and Other True Stories About Friends.* Oxford, OH: H.W. Charles, 1961.

Cleary, Thomas, translator. *Zen Antics: A Hundred Stories of Enlightenment.* Boston, MA: Shambhala Publications, Inc., 1993.

Clemens, Cyril. *Chesterton As Seen by His Contemporaries.* New York: Haskell House Publishers, Ltd., 1969.

Clemens, Cyril. "An Evening with A.E. Housman." Webster Groves, MO: International Mark Twain Society, 1937.

Cole, Joanna. *On the Bus with Joanna Cole.* With Wendy Saul. Portsmouth, NH: Heinemann, 1996.

Collier, Denise, and Kathleen Beckett. *Spare Ribs: Women in the Humor Biz.* New York: St. Martin's Press, 1980.

Datnow, Claire L. *American Science Fiction and Fantasy Writers.* Berkeley Heights, NJ: Enslow Publications, Inc., 1999.

DeCaro, Frank. *A Boy Named Phyllis.* New York: Viking, 1996.

Deedy, John. *A Book of Catholic Anecdotes.* Allen, TX: Thomas More, 1997.

DeMott, Robert J. *Dave Smith: A Literary Archive.* Athens, OH: Ohio University Libraries, 2000.

Dommermuth-Costa, Carol. *Emily Dickinson: Singular Poet.* Minneapolis, MN: Lerner Publications Company, 1998.

Drennan, Robert E., editor. *The Algonquin Wits.* New York: The Citadel Press, 1968.

Ebert, Roger; Daniel Curley, and Jack Lane. *The Perfect London Walk.* Kansas City, MO: Andrews and McMeel, 1986.

Edwards, Susan. *Erma Bombeck: A Life in Humor.* New York: Avon Books, 1997.

Ehlert, Lois. *Under My Nose.* Katonah, New York: Richard C. Owen Publishers, Inc., 1996.

Epstein, Lawrence J. *A Treasury of Jewish Anecdotes.* Northvale, NJ: Jason Aronson, Inc., 1989.

Erlanger, Ellen. *Isaac Asimov: Scientist and Storyteller.* Minneapolis, MN: Lerner Publications Company, 1986.

Farrar, Geraldine. *Such Sweet Compulsion.* New York: The Greystone Press, 1938.

Fine, Edith Hope. *Gary Paulsen: Author and Wilderness Adventurer.* Berkeley Heights, NJ: Enslow Publications, Inc., 2000.

Fonteyn, Margot. *Autobiography.* New York: Alfred A. Knopf, 1976.

Ford, Corey. *The Time of Laughter*. Boston, MA: Little, Brown and Company, 1967.

Ford, Michael Thomas. *Alec Baldwin Doesn't Love Me, and Other Trials from My Queer Life*. Los Angeles, CA: Alyson Books, 1998.

Ford, Michael Thomas. *That's* Mr. Faggot *to You: Further Tales from My Queer Life*. Los Angeles, CA: Alyson Books, 1999.

Gershick, Zsa Zsa. *Gay Old Girls*. Los Angeles, CA: Alyson Books, 1998.

Goodman, Jack, and Albert Rice. *I Wish I'd Said That!* New York: Simon and Schuster, 1935.

Hajdusiewicz, Babs Bell. *Mary Carter Smith: African-American Storyteller*. Springfield, NJ: Enslow Publications, Inc., 1995.

Hall, Marilyn, and Rabbi Jerome Cutler. *The Celebrity Kosher Cookbook*. Los Angeles, CA: J.P. Tarcher, Inc., 1975.

Hanff, Helene. *Q's Legacy*. Boston, MA: Little, Brown and Company, 1985.

Hecht, Ben. *Charlie: The Improbable Life and Times of Charles MacArthur*. New York: Harper & Brothers, Publishers, 1957.

Henry, Lewis C. *Humorous Anecdotes About Famous People*. Garden City, NY: Halcyon House, 1948.

Holland, Merlin. *The Wilde Album*. New York: Henry Holt and Company, 1997.

Irving, Gordon, compiler. *The Wit of the Scots*. London: Leslie Frewin Publishers, Inc., 1969.

Ishizuka, Kathy. *Asian American Authors*. Berkeley Heights, NJ: Enslow Publications, Inc., 2000.

Kolasky, John, collector and compiler. *Look, Comrade — The People are Laughing ....* Toronto, Ontario: Peter Martin Associates Limited, 1972.

Kornfield, Jack, and Christina Feldman. *Soul Food: Stories to Nourish the Spirit and the Heart*. San Francisco, CA: HarperSanFrancisco, 1996. This is a revised edition of their 1991 book *Stories of the Spirit, Stories of the Heart*.

Kovacs, Deborah. *Meet the Authors*. New York: Scholastic Professional Books, 1995.

Kovacs, Deborah, and James Preller. *Meet the Authors and Illustrators*. New York: Scholastic, Inc., 1991.

Lazo, Caroline. *Alice Walker: Freedom Writer*. Minneapolis, MN: Lerner Publications Company, 2000.

Lewis, Mildred and Milton. *Famous Modern Newspaper Writers*. New York: Dodd, Mead & Company, 1962.

Linkletter, Art. *I Wish I'd Said That! My Favorite Ad-Libs of All Time*. Garden City, NY: Doubleday & Co., Inc., 1968.

Lopez, Erika. *Lap Dancing for Mommy: Tender Stories of Disgust, Blame and Inspiration*. Seattle, WA: Seal Press, 1997.

Lowry, Lois. *Looking Back: A Book of Memories*. Boston, MA: Houghton Mifflin Company, 1998.

Madison, Bob. *American Horror Writers*. Berkeley Heights, NJ: Enslow Publications, Inc., 2001.

Mahy, Margaret. *My Mysterious World*. Katonah, NY: Richard C. Owen Publishers, Inc., 1995.

Marcus, Leonard S., compiler and editor. *Author Talk*. New York: Simon and Schuster Books for Young Readers, 2000.

Maverick, Jr., Maury. *Texas Iconoclast*. Edited by Allan O. Kownslar. Fort Worth, TX: Texas Christian University Press, 1997.

McCann, Sean, compiler. *The Wit of the Irish*. Nashville, TN: Aurora Publishers, Ltd., 1970.

McCann, Sean, compiler. *The Wit of Oscar Wilde*. New York: Barnes and Noble, Inc., 1969.

McKissack, Patricia. *Can You Imagine?* Katonah, NY: Richard C. Owen Publishers, Inc., 1997.

McPhail, David. *In Flight with David McPhail*. Katonah, NY: Richard C. Owen Publishers, Inc., 1996.

McPhee, Nancy. *The Book of Insults*. New York: St. Martin's Press, 1978.

McPhee, Nancy. *The Second Book of Insults*. Toronto, Canada: Van Nostrand Reinhold, Ltd., 1981.

Miller, Brandon Marie. *Just What the Doctor Ordered: The History of American Medicine*. Minneapolis, MN: Lerner Publications Company, 1997.

Milton, Steve. *Skate Talk: Figure Skating in the Words of the Stars*. Buffalo, NY: Firefly Books, Inc., 1997.

Moore, Michael. *Stupid White Men*. New York: HarperCollins Publishers, Inc., 2001.

Mostel, Kate, and Madeline Gilford. *170 Years of Show Business*. With Jack Gilford and Zero Mostel. New York: Random House, 1978.

Myers, Walter Dean. *Bad Boy: A Memoir*. New York: HarperCollins Publishers, 2001.

Orleans, Ellen. *Still Can't Keep a Straight Face*. Bala Cynwyd, PA: Laugh Lines Press, 1996.

Patner, Andrew. *I.F. Stone: A Portrait*. New York: Doubleday, 1988.

Paulsen, Gary. *Guts: The True Stories Behind* Hatchet *and the Brian Books*. New York, Delacorte Press, 2001.

Pearson, Hesketh. *Lives of the Wits*. New York: Harper & Row, Publishers, 1962.

Perry, Joel. *Funny That Way: Adventures in Fabulousness*. Los Angeles, CA: Alyson Books, 2001.

Prescott, Orville. *The Five-Dollar Gold Piece*. New York: Random House, 1955.

Presnall, Judith Janda. *Rachel Carson*. San Diego, CA: Lucent Books, 1995.

Primack, Ben, adapter and editor. *The Ben Hecht Show: Impolitic Observations from the Freest Thinker of 1950s Television*. Jefferson, NC: McFarland & Company, Inc., Publishers, 1993.

Ravitch, Diane, editor. *The American Reader: Words That Moved a Nation*. New York: HarperCollins Publishers, 1990.

Rediger, Pat. *Great African Americans in Literature*. New York: Crabtree Publishing Company, 1996.

Richards, Dick, compiler. *The Wit of Noël Coward*. London: Leslie Frewin, 1968.

Richards, Dick, compiler. *The Wit of Peter Ustinov*. London: Leslie Frewin Publishers, Limited, 1969.

Rodriguez-Hunter, Suzanne. *Found Meals of the Lost Generation*. Boston, MA: Faber and Faber, 1994.

Rosten, Leo. *People I Have Loved, Known or Admired*. New York: McGraw-Hill Book Company, 1970.

Rowh, Mark. *W.E.B. Du Bois: Champion of Civil Rights*. Berkeley Heights, NJ: Enslow Publications, Inc., 1999.

Russell, Fred, teller. *Funny Thing About Sports*. Nashville, TN: The McQuiddy Press, 1948.

Russell, Fred. *I'll Try Anything Twice*. Nashville, TN: The McQuiddy Press, 1945.

Rutkowska, Wanda. *Famous People in Anecdotes*. Warszawa: Wydawnictwa Szkolne i Pedagogiczne, 1977.

Saidman, Anne. *Stephen King: Master of Horror*. Minneapolis, MN: Lerner Publications Company, 1992.

Sampson, Edward C. *E.B. White*. New York: Twayne Publishers, 1974.

Sausser, Gail. *Lesbian Etiquette*. Trumansburg, NY: The Crossing Press, 1986.

Scheader, Catherine. *Lorraine Hansberry: Playwright and Voice of Justice*. Springfield, NJ: Enslow Publications, Inc., 1998.

Smaridge, Norah. *Famous Author-Illustrators for Young People*. New York: Dodd, Mead & Company, 1973.

Smaridge, Norah. *Famous Modern Storytellers for Young People*. New York: Dodd, Mead & Company, 1969.

Smith, H. Allen. *Lo, the Former Egyptian!* Garden City, NY: Doubleday & Co., Inc. 1947.

Smith, H. Allen. *To Hell in a Handbasket*. Garden City, NY: Doubleday & Company, Inc., 1962.

Sorel, Nancy Caldwell, and Edward Sorel. *First Encounters: A Book of Memorable Meetings*. New York: Alfred A. Knopf, 1994.

Spinelli, Jerry. *Knots in My Yo-yo String: The Autobiography of a Kid*. New York: Alfred A. Knopf, 1998.

Stine, R.L. *It Came From Ohio: My Life as a Writer*. As told to Joe Arthur. New York: Scholastic, Inc., 1997.

Strickland, Michael R. *African-American Poets*. Springfield, NJ: Enslow Publications, Inc., 1996.

Sullivan, Frank. *Well, There's No Harm in Laughing*. Garden City, NY: Doubleday & Company, Inc., 1970.

Terry-Thomas, and Terry Daum. *Terry-Thomas ... Tells Tales*. London: Robson Books, 1990.

Tingum, Janice. *E.B. White: The Elements of a Writer*. Minneapolis, MN: Lerner Publications Company, 1995.

Tobias, Andrew. *The Best Little Boy in the World Grows Up*. New York: Random House, 1998.

Toklas, Alice. B. *The Alice B. Toklas Cook Book*. Garden City, NY: Anchor Books, 1954.

Troy, Con. *Laugh with Hugh Troy, World's Greatest Practical Joker*. Wyomissing, PA: Trojan Books, 1983.

Turk, Ruth. *Lillian Hellman: Rebel Playwright*. Minneapolis, MN: Lerner Publications Company, 1995.

Twain, Mark. *The Oxford Mark Twain*. New York: Oxford University Press, 1996. This is a complete set of the works of Mark Twain.

Wadsworth, Ginger. *Laura Ingalls Wilder: Storyteller of the Prairie*. Minneapolis, MN: Lerner Publications Company, 1997.

Wasserman, Harriet. *Handsome Is: Adventures with Saul Bellow*. New York: Fromm International Publishing Company, 1997.

Weidt, Maryann N. *Oh, the Places He Went: A Story About Dr. Seuss*. Minneapolis, MN: Carolrhoda Books, Inc., 1994.

West, Mark I. *Roald Dahl*. New York: Twayne Publishers, 1992.

Wilkinson, Brenda. *African American Women Writers*. New York: John Wiley and Sons, Inc., 2000.

Williams, Kenneth. *Acid Drops*. London: J. M. Dent & Sons, Ltd., 1980.

Wilson, Suzan. *Stephen King: King of Thrillers and Horror*. Berkeley Heights, NJ: Enslow Publications, Inc., 2000.

Woog, Dan. *Dear Dan ... Apologies From an Imperfect World*. Los Angeles, CA: Alyson Books, 2001.

Woolf, Vicki. *Dancing in the Vortex: The Story of Ida Rubinstein*. Australia: Harwood Academic Publishers, 2000.

Wyer, Malcolm Glenn. *Books and People: Short Anecdotes from a Long Experience*. Denver, CO: The Old West Publishing Co., 1964.

Appendix B: About the Author

It was a dark and stormy night. Suddenly a cry rang out, and on a hot summer night in 1954, Josephine, wife of Carl Bruce, gave birth to a boy — me. Unfortunately, this young married couple allowed Reuben Saturday, Josephine's brother, to name their first-born. Reuben, aka "The Joker," decided that Bruce was a nice name, so he decided to name me Bruce Bruce. I have gone by my middle name — David — ever since.

Being named Bruce David Bruce hasn't been all bad. Bank tellers remember me very quickly, so I don't often have to show an ID. It can be fun in charades, also. When I was a counselor as a teenager at Camp Echoing Hills in Warsaw, Ohio, a fellow counselor gave the signs for "sounds like" and "two words," then she pointed to a bruise on her leg twice. Bruise Bruise? Oh yeah, Bruce Bruce is the answer!

Uncle Reuben, by the way, gave me a haircut when I was in kindergarten. He cut my hair short and shaved a small bald spot on the back of my head. My mother wouldn't let me go to school until the bald spot grew out again.

Of all my brothers and sisters (six in all), I am the only transplant to Athens, Ohio. I was born in Newark, Ohio, and have lived all around Southeastern Ohio. However, I moved to Athens to go to Ohio University and have never left.

At Ohio U, I never could make up my mind whether to major in English or Philosophy, so I got a bachelor's degree with a double major in both areas, then I added a Master of Arts degree in English and a Master of Arts degree in Philosophy. Yes, I have my MAMA degree.

Currently, and for a long time to come (I eat fruits and veggies), I am spending my retirement writing books such as *Nadia Comaneci: Perfect 10*, *The Funniest People in Comedy*, *Homer's* Iliad: *A Retelling in Prose*, and *William Shakespeare's* Hamlet: *A Retelling in Prose*.

By the way, my sister Brenda Kennedy writes romances such as *A New Beginning* and *Shattered Dreams*.

Appendix C: Some Books by David Bruce

Anecdote Collections

250 Anecdotes About Opera

250 Anecdotes About Religion

250 Anecdotes About Religion: Volume 2

250 Music Anecdotes

Be a Work of Art: 250 Anecdotes and Stories

The Coolest People in Art: 250 Anecdotes

The Coolest People in the Arts: 250 Anecdotes

The Coolest People in Books: 250 Anecdotes

The Coolest People in Comedy: 250 Anecdotes

Create, Then Take a Break: 250 Anecdotes

Don't Fear the Reaper: 250 Anecdotes

The Funniest People in Art: 250 Anecdotes

The Funniest People in Books: 250 Anecdotes

The Funniest People in Books, Volume 2: 250 Anecdotes

The Funniest People in Books, Volume 3: 250 Anecdotes

The Funniest People in Comedy: 250 Anecdotes

The Funniest People in Dance: 250 Anecdotes

The Funniest People in Families: 250 Anecdotes

The Funniest People in Families, Volume 2: 250 Anecdotes

The Funniest People in Families, Volume 3: 250 Anecdotes

The Funniest People in Families, Volume 4: 250 Anecdotes

The Funniest People in Families, Volume 5: 250 Anecdotes

The Funniest People in Families, Volume 6: 250 Anecdotes

The Funniest People in Movies: 250 Anecdotes

The Funniest People in Music: 250 Anecdotes

The Funniest People in Music, Volume 2: 250 Anecdotes

The Funniest People in Music, Volume 3: 250 Anecdotes

The Funniest People in Neighborhoods: 250 Anecdotes

The Funniest People in Relationships: 250 Anecdotes

The Funniest People in Sports: 250 Anecdotes

The Funniest People in Sports, Volume 2: 250 Anecdotes

The Funniest People in Television and Radio: 250 Anecdotes

The Funniest People in Theater: 250 Anecdotes

The Funniest People Who Live Life: 250 Anecdotes

The Funniest People Who Live Life, Volume 2: 250 Anecdotes

The Kindest People Who Do Good Deeds, Volume 1: 250 Anecdotes

The Kindest People Who Do Good Deeds, Volume 2: 250 Anecdotes

Maximum Cool: 250 Anecdotes

The Most Interesting People in Movies: 250 Anecdotes

The Most Interesting People in Politics and History: 250 Anecdotes

The Most Interesting People in Politics and History, Volume 2: 250 Anecdotes

The Most Interesting People in Politics and History, Volume 3: 250 Anecdotes

The Most Interesting People in Religion: 250 Anecdotes

The Most Interesting People in Sports: 250 Anecdotes

The Most Interesting People Who Live Life: 250 Anecdotes

The Most Interesting People Who Live Life, Volume 2: 250 Anecdotes

Reality is Fabulous: 250 Anecdotes and Stories

Resist Psychic Death: 250 Anecdotes

Seize the Day: 250 Anecdotes and Stories

---

[1] Source: Everett S. Allen, *Famous American Humorous Poets*, p. 27.

[2] Source: André Bernard, *Now All We Need is a Title*, p. 126.

[3] Source: Suzan Wilson, *Stephen King: King of Thrillers and Horror*, p. 63.

[4] Source: Lewis C. Henry, *Humorous Anecdotes About Famous People*, pp. 62-63.

[5] Source: Roger Ebert and Daniel Curley, *The Perfect London Walk*, p. xii.

[6] Source: Mark Twain, *A Tramp Abroad*, Oxford Mark Twain, p. 614.

[7] Source: Franklin P. Adams, et. al., *Percy Hammond: A Symposium in Tribute*, p. viii.

[8] Source: Edith Hope Fine, *Gary Paulsen: Author and Wilderness Adventurer*, pp. 38-39.

[9] Source: Janice Tingum, *E.B. White: The Elements of a Writer*, pp. 93-94, 103.

[10] Source: Ginger Wadsworth, *Laura Ingalls Wilder: Storyteller of the Prairie*, p. 26.

[11] Source: Carmen Bredeson, *American Writers of the 20th Century*, p. 53.

[12] Source: Susan Edwards, *Erma Bombeck*, p. 172.

[13] Source: Bob Madison, *American Horror Writers*, pp. 69, 71.

[14] Source: Suzan Wilson, *Stephen King: King of Thrillers and Horror*, pp. 78-79.

[15] Source: Paul Bailey, editor, *The Stately Homo: A Celebration of the Life of Quentin Crisp*, p. 149.

[16] Source: Harriet Wasserman, *Handsome Is: Adventures with Saul Bellow*, p. 122.

[17] Source: Michael Moore, *Stupid White Men*, pp. 123-124.

[18] Source: Peg Bracken, *I Didn't Come Here to Argue*, p. 41.

[19] Source: David McPhail, *In Flight with David McPhail*, p. 10.

[20] Source: Ruth Turk, *Lillian Hellman: Rebel Playwright*, p. 30.

[21] Source: Orville Prescott, *The Five-Dollar Gold Piece*, p. 61.

[22] Source: Cyril Clemens, "An Evening with A.E. Housman," p. 13.

[23] Source: Brandon Marie Miller, *Just What the Doctor Ordered: The History of American Medicine*, p. 40.

[24] Source: Roy Blount, Jr., "Introduction" to Mark Twain's *Celebrated Jumping Frog of Calaveras County*, Oxford Mark Twain, p. xliv.

[25] Source: Sean McCann, compiler, *The Wit of Oscar Wilde*, pp. 99-100.

[26] Source: Mark Rowh, *W E B. Du Bois: Champion of Civil Rights*, pp. 94-97, 99, 101.

[27] Source: Suzanne Rodriguez-Hunter, *Found Meals of the Lost Generation*, pp. 34-35, 67.

[28] Source: John Kolasky, collector and compiler, *Look, Comrade — The People are Laughing ...*, p. 115.

[29] Source: Margot Fonteyn, *Autobiography*, p. 58.

[30] Source: Angelica Shirley Carpenter and Jean Shirley, *L. Frank Baum: Royal Historian of Oz*, pp. 133-134.

[31] Source: Suzanne Rodriguez-Hunter, *Found Meals of the Lost Generation*, pp. 210-211.

[32] Source: Kathy Ishizuka, *Asian American Authors*, p. 91.

[33] Source: Orville Prescott, *The Five-Dollar Gold Piece*, p. ix.

[34] Source: Ruth Turk, *Lillian Hellman: Rebel Playwright*, p. 28.

[35] Source: Con Troy, *Laugh with Hugh Troy*, p. 124.

[36] Source: Claire L. Datnow, *American Science Fiction and Fantasy Writers*, p. 84.

[37] Source: Diane Ravitch, editor, *The American Reader*, pp. 63-64.

[38] Source: Merlin Holland, *The Wilde Album*, p. 117.

[39] Source: Norah Smaridge, *Famous Author-Illustrators for Young People*, p. 83.

[40] Source: Patricia McKissack, *Can You Imagine?*, p. 5.

[41] Source: Carmen Bredeson, *American Writers of the 20th Century*, p. 27.

[42] Source: Angelica Shirley Carpenter and Jean Shirley, *L. Frank Baum: Royal Historian of Oz*, p. 85.

[43] Source: Michael Bronski, consulting editor, *Outstanding Lives*, p. 18.

[44] Source: John Deedy, *A Book of Catholic Anecdotes*, p. 29.

[45] Source: Carol Dommermuth-Costa, *Emily Dickinson: Singular Poet*, p. 36.

[46] Source: Jerry Spinelli, *Knots in My Yo-yo String: The Autobiography of a Kid*, pp. 69-70.

[47] Source: Terry-Thomas and Terry Daum, *Terry-Thomas Tells Tales*, p. 64.

[48] Source: Denise Collier and Kathleen Beckett, *Spare Ribs*, p. 23.

[49] Source: Lois Lowry, *Looking Back: A Book of Memories*, pp. 141-143.

[50] Source: Mildred and Milton Lewis, *Famous Modern Newspaper Writers*, pp. 41-42.

[51] Source: Bob Madison, *American Horror Writers*, pp. 60-61.

[52] Source: Kate Mostel and Madeline Gilford, *170 Years of Show Business*, p. x.

[53] Source: H. Allen Smith, *To Hell in a Handbasket*, pp. 101-102.

[54] Source: Joey Adams, *The God Bit*, p. 321.

[55] Source: Corey Ford, *The Time of Laughter*, pp. 102-103.

[56] Source: Hesketh Pearson, *Lives of the Wits*, p. 309.

[57] Source: Denise Collier and Kathleen Beckett, *Spare Ribs*, p. 205.

[58] Source: Deborah Kovacs and James Preller, *Meet the Authors and Illustrators*, p. 35.

[59] Source: John Kolasky, collector and compiler, *Look, Comrade — The People are Laughing ...*, p. 115.

[60] Source: Margot Fonteyn, *Autobiography*, p. 245.

[61] Source: Nancy McPhee, *The Book of Insults*, p. 80.

[62] Source: Nancy McPhee, *The Second Book of Insults*, p. 86.

[63] Source: Jack Goodman and Albert Rice, *I Wish I'd Said That!*, p. 98.

[64] Source: Mark Twain, *Innocents Abroad*, Oxford Mark Twain, pp. 292, 294-295, 302.

[65] Source: Mark I. West, *Roald Dahl*, p. 8.

[66] Source: Helen Chappell, *The Chesapeake Book of the Dead*, p. 79.

[67] Source: Gary Paulsen, *Guts: The True Stories Behind* Hatchet *and the Brian Books*, p. 115.

[68] Source: Ben Hecht, *Charlie: The Improbable Life and Times of Charles MacArthur*, p. 96.

[69] Source: Gordon Irving, compiler, *The Wit of the Scots*, p. 21.

[70] Source: Part Rediger, *Great African Americans in Literature*, pp. 26-27.

[71] Source: Paul Bailey, editor, *The Stately Homo: A Celebration of the Life of Quentin Crisp*, pp. 146-147.

[72] Source: Geraldine Farrar, *Such Sweet Compulsion*, p. 3.

[73] Source: George Plimpton, "Introduction" to Mark Twain's *Roughing It*, Oxford Mark Twain, p. xxxvi.

[74] Source: Roger Ebert and Daniel Curley, *The Perfect London Walk*, p. 102.

[75] Source: Sean McCann, compiler, *The Wit of the Irish*, p. 97.

[76] Source: H. Allen Smith, *To Hell in a Handbasket*, p. 319.

[77] Source: Nancy McPhee, *The Book of Insults*, p. 81.

[78] Source: Wanda Rutkowska, *Famous People in Anecdotes*, pp. 13-14.

[79] Source: Helen White Charles, collector and editor, *Quaker Chuckles*, p. 102.

[80] Source: Helene Hanff, *Q's Legacy*, pp. 4-5.

[81] Source: Mark Twain, *Life on the Mississippi*, Oxford Mark Twain, pp. 159ff.

[82] Source: Catherine Scheader, *Lorraine Hansberry: Playwright and Voice of Justice*, pp. 35-36, 76.

[83] Source: Walter Dean Myers, *Bad Boy: A Memoir*, pp. 56-57.

[84] Source: Corey Ford, *The Time of Laughter*, pp. 16-17.

[85] Source: Mark Twain, *A Tramp Abroad*, the Oxford Mark Twain, p. 45.

[86] Source: Janice Tingum, *E.B. White: The Elements of a Writer*, p. 40.

[87] Source: Nathaniel Benchley, *Robert Benchley*, p. 47.

[88] Source: Robert J. DeMott, *Dave Smith: A Literary Archive*, p. 2.

[89] Source: Michael Moore, *Stupid White Men*, pp. 92, 95.

[90] Source: Peg Bracken, *I Didn't Come Here to Argue*, p. 149.

[91] Source: Ginger Wadsworth, *Laura Ingalls Wilder: Storyteller of the Prairie*, p. 31.

[92] Source: H. Allen Smith, *Lo, the Former Egyptian!*, p. 62.

[93] Source: Leo Rosten, *People I Have Loved, Known or Admired*, p. 24.

[94] Source: Jack Kornfield and Christina Feldman, *Soul Food*, p. 194.

[95] Source: Deborah Kovacs, *Meet the Authors*, p. 20.

[96] Source: Judith Janda Presnall, *Rachel Carson*, p. 47.

[97] Source: Helen White Charles, collector and editor, *Quaker Chuckles*, pp. 7-8.

[98] Source: Michèle Brown and Ann O'Connor, *Hammer and Tongues*, p. 115.

[99] Source: R.L. Stine, *It Came From Ohio: My Life as a Writer*, pp. 125-126.

[100] Source: Frank DeCaro, *A Boy Named Phyllis*, pp. 42-43.

[101] Source: Lawrence J. Epstein, *A Treasury of Jewish Anecdotes*, p. 20.

[102] Source: Leo Rosten, *People I Have Loved, Known or Admired*, p. 24.

[103] Source: Gary Paulsen, *Guts: The True Stories Behind* Hatchet *and the Brian Books*, pp. 129-134.

[104] Source: Brandon Marie Miller, *Just What the Doctor Ordered: The History of American Medicine*, p. 70.

[105] Source: Part Rediger, *Great African Americans in Literature*, p. 26.

[106] Source: Willis Barnstone, translator, *Greek Lyric Poetry*, p. 154.

[107] Source: Michael Thomas Ford, *That's* Mr. Faggot *to You*, p. 5.

[108] Source: Erma Bombeck, *I Want to Grow Hair, I Want to Grow Up, I Want to Go to Boise*, p. 45.

[109] Source: Maryann N. Weidt, *Oh, the Places He Went: A Story About Dr. Seuss*, p. 45.

[110] Source: Marilyn Hall and Rabbi Jerome Cutler, *The Celebrity Kosher Cookbook*, p. 27.

[111] Source: Alice B. Toklas, *The Alice B. Toklas Cook Book*, pp. 273-274.

[112] Source: Michael Thomas Ford, *Alec Baldwin Doesn't Love Me*, pp. 176ff.

[113] Source: Andrew Tobias, *The Best Little Boy in the World Grows Up*, pp. 25-26.

[114] Source: Ellen Orleans, *Still Can't Keep a Straight Face*, pp. 99-100.

[115] Source: Frank DeCaro, *A Boy Named Phyllis*, pp. 110-111.

[116] Source: Erika Lopez, *Lap Dancing for Mommy*, p. 99.

[117] Source: Gail Sausser, *Lesbian Etiquette*, p. 93.

[118] Source: Hesketh Pearson, *Lives of the Wits*, p. 242.

[119] Source: Judy Carter, *The Homo Handbook*, p. 187.

[120] Source: Vicki Woolf, *Dancing in the Vortex: The Story of Ida Rubinstein*, p. 107.

[121] Source: Jack Goodman and Albert Rice, *I Wish I'd Said That!*, p. 105.

[122] Source: Vicki Woolf, *Dancing in the Vortex: The Story of Ida Rubinstein*, p. 140.

[123] Source: Anne Saidman, *Stephen King: Master of Horror*, pp. 22-23.

[124] Source: Erma Bombeck, *I Want to Grow Hair, I Want to Grow Up, I Want to Go to Boise*, pp. 12-13.

[125] Source: Cyril Clemens, *Chesterton As Seen by His Contemporaries*, p. 167.

[126] Source: Joanna Cole, *On the Bus with Joanna Cole*, p. 44.

[127] Source: Norah Smaridge, *Famous Author-Illustrators for Young People*, p. 70.

[128] Source: Franklin P. Adams, et. al., *Percy Hammond: A Symposium in Tribute*, pp. 60-62.

[129] Source: Kenneth Williams, *Acid Drops*, p. 65.

[130] Source: Cyril Clemens, *Chesterton As Seen by His Contemporaries*, p. 28.

[131] Source: Nancy McPhee, *The Second Book of Insults*, pp. 36-37.

[132] Source: Sean McCann, compiler, *The Wit of Oscar Wilde*, p. 9.

[133] Source: Ivar Bryce, *You Only Live Once*, pp. 126-127.

[134] Source: Kenneth Williams, *Acid Drops*, p. 83.

[135] Source: Art Linkletter, *I Wish I'd Said That!*, p. 34.

[136] Source: Fred Russell, *I'll Try Anything Twice*, p. 91.

[137] Source: Mark Twain, *Innocents Abroad*, Oxford Mark Twain, p. 134.

[138] Source: Andrew Patner, *I.F. Stone: A Portrait*, p. 130.

[139] Source: Babs Bell Hajdusiewicz, *Mary Carter Smith: African-American Storyteller*, p. 23.

[140] Source: Cyril Clemens, "An Evening with A.E. Housman," p. 18.

[141] Source: Art Linkletter, *I Wish I'd Said That!*, p. 60.

[142] Source: Mordecai Richler, "Introduction" to Mark Twain's *Innocents Abroad*, Oxford Mark Twain, p. xxxi.

[143] Source: Dan Woog, *Dear Dan ... Apologies From an Imperfect World*, "Introduction" and pp. 1-3.

[144] Source: Deborah Kovacs and James Preller, *Meet the Authors and Illustrators*, p. 55.

[145] Source: Robert E. Drennan, editor, *The Algonquin Wits*, pp. 157-158.

[146] Source: R.L. Stine, *It Came From Ohio: My Life as a Writer*, p. 118.

[147] Source: Ellen Orleans, *Still Can't Keep a Straight Face*, p. 100.

[148] Source: Lewis C. Henry, *Humorous Anecdotes About Famous People*, p. 127.

[149] Source: Ben Primack, adapter and editor, *The Ben Hecht Show*, p. 29.

[150] Source: H. Allen Smith, *Lo, the Former Egyptian!*, p. 105.

[151] Source: Ben Primack, adapter and editor, *The Ben Hecht Show*, p. 24.

[152] Source: Helen Chappell, *The Chesapeake Book of the Dead*, pp. 53, 55.

[153] Source: Ben Hecht, *Charlie: The Improbable Life and Times of Charles MacArthur*, pp. 43-44.

[154] Source: Malcolm Glenn Wyer, *Books and People*, pp. 116-117.

[155] Source: Con Troy, *Laugh with Hugh Troy*, p. 147.

[156] Source: Marc Connelly, "Introduction" to Frank Sullivan's *Well, There's No Harm in Laughing*, p. xi.

[157] Source: Maury Maverick, Jr., *Texas Iconoclast*, pp. 58-59.

[158] Source: Everett S. Allen, *Famous American Humorous Poets*, p. 47.

[159] Source: Fred Russell, *I'll Try Anything Twice*, p. 90.

[160] Source: Peg Bracken, *But I Wouldn't Have Missed It for the World!*, pp. 144-145.

[161] Source: Mark Twain, *Celebrated Jumping Frog of Calaveras County*, Oxford Mark Twain, dedication.

[162] Source: Zsa Zsa Gershick, *Gay Old Girls*, pp. 186-187.

[163] Source: Mordecai Richler, "Introduction" to Mark Twain's *Innocents Abroad*, Oxford Mark Twain, pp. xxxix-xl.

[164] Source: Anne Saidman, *Stephen King: Master of Horror*, p. 49.

[165] Source: Dick Richards, compiler, *The Wit of Noël Coward*, p. 33.

[166] Source: Sean McCann, compiler, *The Wit of the Irish*, p. 125.

[167] Source: Joel Perry, *Funny That Way: Adventures in Fabulousness*, pp. 24-25.

[168] Source: Nancy Caldwell Sorel and Edward Sorel, *First Encounters*, p. 93.

[169] Source: Marilyn Hall and Rabbi Jerome Cutler, *The Celebrity Kosher Cookbook*, p. 117.

[170] Source: Merlin Holland, *The Wilde Album*, pp. 19-20.

[171] Source: Susan Edwards, *Erma Bombeck*, p. 134.

[172] Source: Erika Lopez, *Lap Dancing for Mommy*, p. 87.

[173] Source: Gail Sausser, *Lesbian Etiquette*, p. 40.

[174] Source: Michael Thomas Ford, *That's* Mr. Faggot *to You*, p. 234.

[175] Source: Geraldine Farrar, *Such Sweet Compulsion*, p. 204.

[176] Source: Edward C. Sampson, *E.B. White*, p. 29.

[177] Source: Ivar Bryce, *You Only Live Once*, pp. 96-97.

[178] Source: Ellen Erlanger, *Isaac Asimov: Scientist and Storyteller*, p. 49.

[179] Source: Claire L. Datnow, *American Science Fiction and Fantasy Writers*, p. 75.

[180] Source: Harriet Wasserman, *Handsome Is: Adventures with Saul Bellow*, p. 60.

[181] Source: J. Bryan III, *Merry Gentlemen (and One Lady)*, pp. 189-190.

[182] Source: Robert E. Drennan, editor, *The Algonquin Wits*, p. 122.

[183] Source: Susan Bivin Aller, *J.M. Barrie: The Magic Behind Peter Pan*, pp. 107, 109.

[184] Source: Caroline Lazo, *Alice Walker: Freedom Writer*, pp. 84-85.

[185] Source: Dick Richards, compiler, *The Wit of Peter Ustinov*, pp. 20-21.

[186] Source: Robert E. Drennan, editor, *The Algonquin Wits*, pp. 141.

[187] Source: Kate Mostel and Madeline Gilford, *170 Years of Show Business*, p. 6.

[188] Source: Dick Richards, compiler, *The Wit of Noël Coward*, p. 20.

[189] Source: Michael Bronski, consulting editor, *Outstanding Lives*, p. 194.

[190] Source: Michael R. Strickland, *African-American Poets*, p. 31.

[191] Source: Robert J. DeMott, *Dave Smith: A Literary Archive*, pp. 20-21.

[192] Source: Nancy Caldwell Sorel and Edward Sorel, *First Encounters*, p. 73.

[193] Source: Gordon Irving, compiler, *The Wit of the Scots*, p. 17.

[194] Source: Carol Dommermuth-Costa, *Emily Dickinson: Singular Poet*, pp. 23-24, 71.

[195] Source: Norah Smaridge, *Famous Modern Storytellers for Young People*, p. 93.

[196] Source: Malcolm Glenn Wyer, *Books and People*, pp. 118-119.

[197] Source: Mark Twain, *Roughing It*, Oxford Mark Twain, pp. 102-103.

[198] Source: Fred Russell, teller, *Funny Thing About Sports*, p. 91.

[199] Source: George Oppenheimer, "Afterword" to Frank Sullivan's *Well, There's No Harm in Laughing*, p. 258.

[200] Source: Catherine Scheader, *Lorraine Hansberry: Playwright and Voice of Justice*, pp. 18, 20-22.

[201] Source: Babs Bell Hajdusiewicz, *Mary Carter Smith: African-American Storyteller*, pp. 7-9, 16.

[202] Source: Brenda Wilkinson, *African American Women Writers*, pp. 37-38.

[203] Source: Michael R. Strickland, *African-American Poets*, p. 58.

[204] Source: Maury Maverick, Jr., *Texas Iconoclast*, p. 231.

[205] Source: Judith Janda Presnall, *Rachel Carson*, pp. 45-46.

[206] Source: Andrew Patner, *I.F. Stone: A Portrait*, p. 123.

[207] Source: Lawrence J. Epstein, *A Treasury of Jewish Anecdotes*, p. 102.

[208] Source: Mark Rowh, *W.E.B. Du Bois: Champion of Civil Rights*, p. 28.

[209] Source: Mildred and Milton Lewis, *Famous Modern Newspaper Writers*, pp. 34-35.

[210] Source: Jerry Spinelli, *Knots in My Yo-yo String: The Autobiography of a Kid*, pp. 134-135.

[211] Source: Deborah Kovacs, *Meet the Authors*, pp. 45-46.

[212] Source: Leonard S. Marcus, compiler and editor, *Author Talk*, p. 73.

[213] Source: Helene Hanff, *Q's Legacy*, p. 117.

[214] Source: Caroline Lazo, *Alice Walker: Freedom Writer*, p. 40.

[215] Source: Kathy Ishizuka, *Asian American Authors*, p. 38.

[216] Source: Joanna Cole, *On the Bus with Joanna Cole*, pp. 20-21.

[217] Source: Dick Richards, compiler, *The Wit of Peter Ustinov*, p. 34.

[218] Source: Michael Thomas Ford, *Alec Baldwin Doesn't Love Me*, pp. 137-139.

[219] Source: Willis Barnstone, translator, *Greek Lyric Poetry*, p. 113.

[220] Source: Zsa Zsa Gershick, *Gay Old Girls*, p. 168.

[221] Source: Susan Bivin Aller, *J.M. Barrie: The Magic Behind Peter Pan*, pp. 37-38.

[222] Source: Fred Russell, teller, *Funny Thing About Sports*, pp. 89-90.

[223] Source: Michèle Brown and Ann O'Connor, *Hammer and Tongues*, p. 85.

[224] Source: Walter Dean Myers, *Bad Boy: A Memoir*, pp. 52-53.

[225] Source: Steve Milton, *Skate Talk: Figure Skating in the Words of the Stars*, p. 207.

[226] Source: Joel Perry, *Funny That Way: Adventures in Fabulousness*, p. 143.

[227] Source: Lois Lowry, *Looking Back: A Book of Memories*, pp. 137-138.

[228] Source: Steve Milton, *Skate Talk: Figure Skating in the Words of the Stars*, p. 28.

[229] Source: André Bernard, *Now All We Need is a Title*, pp. 48, 50.

[230] Source: Andrew Tobias, *The Best Little Boy in the World Grows Up*, p. 216.

[231] Source: Maryann N. Weidt, *Oh, the Places He Went: A Story About Dr. Seuss*, p. 46.

[232] Source: Mark Twain, *Innocents Abroad*, Oxford Mark Twain, p. 291.

[233] Source: Norah Smaridge, *Famous Modern Storytellers for Young People*, pp. 63, 65-66.

[234] Source: Thomas Cleary, translator, *Zen Antics*, p. 17.

[235] Source: Edward C. Sampson, *E.B. White*, pp. 28-29.

[236] Source: Mark Twain, *Innocents Abroad*, Oxford Mark Twain, p. 173.

[237] Source: Leonard S. Marcus, compiler and editor, *Author Talk*, p. 45.

[238] Source: Peg Bracken, *But I Wouldn't Have Missed It for the World!*, p. 10.

[239] Source: Wanda Rutkowska, *Famous People in Anecdotes*, p. 19.

[240] Source: Mark Twain, *Roughing It*, Oxford Mark Twain, p. 258.

[241] Source: John Deedy, *A Book of Catholic Anecdotes*, p. 56.

[242] Source: David McPhail, *In Flight with David McPhail*, pp. 6-7.

[243] Source: Nathaniel Benchley, *Robert Benchley*, p. 183.

[244] Source: Brenda Wilkinson, *African American Women Writers*, pp. 48, 52.

[245] Source: Lois Ehlert, *Under My Nose*, pp. 16-17.

[246] Source: Edith Hope Fine, *Gary Paulsen: Author and Wilderness Adventurer*, p. 48.

[247] Source: Eve Bunting, *Once Upon a Time*, p. 22.

[248] Source: Margaret Mahy, *My Mysterious World*, pp. 25-26.

[249] Source: Ellen Erlanger, *Isaac Asimov: Scientist and Storyteller*, p. 7.

[250] Source: J. Bryan III, *Merry Gentlemen (and One Lady)*, p. 250.

www.ingramcontent.com/pod-product-compliance
Lightning Source LLC
Chambersburg PA
CBHW021006180726
47993CB00017B/1079